MAX FACTOR
AND HOLLYWOOD
A Glamorous History

ERIKA THOMAS | Photos by Marc Wanamaker

THE
History
PRESS

Published by The History Press
Charleston, SC
www.historypress.net

First published 2016

Manufactured in the United States

ISBN 978.1.46713.610.5

Library of Congress Control Number: 2016948314

CONTENTS

PREFACE

Imagine the immense radius that comprises Los Angeles today. Then imagine that before the days of the motorcar or trolley car and before any freeways were in place, Max Factor would pedal on his bicycle—cosmetics and wigs in tow—over pastoral terrain some thirty miles out to the San Fernando Valley and locales beyond to sell his wares to the likes of Cecile B. DeMille and the many pioneering producers like him. It becomes clear, the painstaking work that went into every tube of Supreme Greasepaint, pot of Lip Pomade and sumptuous set of eyelashes Factor would so exquisitely engineer. His immense passion and dedication would cause him to become a major success in Hollywood and, subsequently, throughout the world, and he would set the standard by which an entire industry would operate for more than a century to come. Max Factor didn't just invent glamour. He pioneered the everyday use of commercial cosmetics, taking them from being utterly disdained to widely celebrated around the world.

Envision the excitement the moviegoing public had upon seeing their favorite stars onscreen and in fan magazines like *Motion Picture* and *Photoplay*. In the early years, aside from movies and magazines, all that the public had was imagination. There were no paparazzi, no television or social media, no way to access information by the ton like we do today. There were only the iconic faces of movie stars, projected onto a vast, luminescent screen, and the beauty created by Max Factor.

Marc Wanamaker provided the images for this book. It was a pleasure working with such an expert and someone whose knowledge of Hollywood and Los Angeles history is boundless. Many a time, I've e-mailed him in a pinch, in need of specific high-resolution vintage images for one of the magazines I freelance for. And my requests have run the gamut—from a World War II–era Burbank Airport or a bikini-clad Annette Funicello on the beach in Malibu to Frank Sinatra at Capitol Records and Marilyn Monroe boarding an American Airlines flight at LAX. No matter what the request, he seems to have every photograph of every person within his immense collection. From trolley cars to movie studios to location filming, nobody knows more about Los Angeles history than Marc.

It was also a pleasure working with Jaclyn Smith, who was such an iconic part of Max Factor ad campaigns throughout the 1970s and '80s. In one conversation with her, she referenced her unforgettable Epris commercial, saying, "Part of the art of being a woman is knowing when not to be too much of a lady," as if she were on television leaning confidently on her elbow, one hand resting in her trademark thick brown waves. As hard as it is to think of the stunning actress without *Charlie's Angels* immediately coming to mind, Smith shared with me that she started appearing in Max Factor campaigns before she was ever cast on the show. She also shared with me how much the iconic looks Max Factor first invented influence her personal style to this day and that Hollywood has yet to recapture that mystique.

The famed Max Factor Makeup Studio was more than a landmark. It was a virtual glamour factory—a place that headquartered beauty, where color cosmetics were manufactured, packaged and shipped to all corners of the globe for adoring fans of Max Factor, makeup and the movies. When Donelle Dadigan purchased the dilapidated building, she would singlehandedly save the historic structure from what would have more than likely been an ill fate and, in the process, curate the most renowned collection of beauty artifacts and memorabilia in the world. Thanks to her meticulous work, the Hollywood Museum remains a beacon of glamour and a symbol of Hollywood's halcyon golden era.

Thank you to the fabulous Ms. Debbie Reynolds for sharing her experience with the makeup guru at what was a pivotal time for motion pictures and Max Factor and Company alike and to Richard Adkins at the Hollywood Heritage Museum for imparting his knowledge about the evolution of movie making. Endless thanks to my husband, Frank, and our children, Sydney and Kellen, for continually supporting me in my creative endeavors.

INTRODUCTION

It was from his Highland Avenue glamour factory that the "Father of Modern Makeup" would not only birth innumerable beauty innovations but would also create signature looks for some of the most beautiful women in Hollywood, catapulting them to superstardom and causing the whole world to emulate them.

The landmark building where unprecedented beauty trails were blazed operated as a virtual mini city for decades. It was the place where cosmetics were conceived, designed, manufactured, distributed and retailed. It was where starlets on the verge of major fame came to have their careers launched, and after a time, it would be where all women could and would go to get some glamour.

Prior to Max Factor introducing his makeup line to the public, "paint," if ever worn by a woman on the street, was something to be gravely admonished. After all, this was during the prudish, conservative post-Victorian era and at a time when purity was the ideal personification of what it meant to be feminine. Coventry Patmore's nineteenth-century poem "The Angel in the House" still reflected the societal ideals and expectations of women. Moral women did not paint their faces.

But Max Factor would change the world's perception in an epic way, beginning first with Hollywood, turning the tide of what it meant to look and feel attractive and what it meant to be female—liberating women and creating an entire industry in the process. Did Max Factor know he would come to build something of such lasting phenomenon at the time? Though it was his desire for his business to be successful, it wasn't likely that he did. One thing is for certain, however: the man who began his career sewing costumes for the opera in his home country of Russia would carry out his passion and innate talent for innovating the aesthetically pleasing as if he were born to do nothing else.

Max Factor did more than apply makeup to the faces of Hollywood. In fact, he invented glamour. Without him, the cosmetics industry as we know it today would never have come into existence. This book is not only homage to the many accomplishments of a beauty pioneer, but it is also one to the golden era of Hollywood, which the man himself created. It is a reminder to celebrate glamour. Enjoy this book and all of the glorious vintage images and beauty tips within it. Keep a copy on your night table, give it as a gift to a fellow beauty lover—and never forget to be glamorous.

A publicity photo of Max Factor and Kathleen Burke in 1936. Paramount Studios sponsored a casting contest in the summer of 1932. The dental assistant turned dramatic actress from Chicago beat out sixty thousand hopefuls, winning the role of "Panther Woman" in the science fiction thriller *Island of Lost Souls*. In this image, Burke demonstrates Max Factor cosmetics while the bespectacled makeup guru looks on.

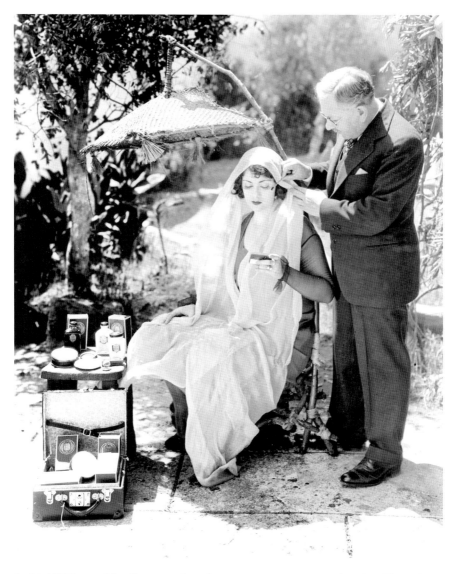

In this 1927 image, Max Factor applies cake mascara to an actress on location. The makeup kit pictured on the left was typical of the ones Factor and his trained artists made available to actors.

"You are not born glamorous.
Glamour is created."
—Max Factor

A super-platinum Jean Harlow during the 1930s. The actress's hair color was so sought after that producer Howard Hughes cashed in on the popularity by offering upward of $10,000 in a contest to the first hairdresser who could re-create the color. Harlow's shade was so much in demand that peroxide sales skyrocketed when women everywhere tried to create their own versions at home.

Actress Nita Naldi during the 1920s at the peak of her career.

Brooklyn-born jazz icon Lena Horne began her career as a chorus girl at the Cotton Club in 1933. In the 1940s, Horne would make her way to Hollywood, where she signed a seven-year contract with MGM. When her studio loaned her to 20th Century Fox to star in the all–African American musical *Stormy Weather*, Max Factor formulated Light Egyptian, a makeup to complement her already stunning complexion. *Stormy Weather* would become one of the most popular films of the era, with its title song serving as Horne's signature musical number for the rest of her career.

Chapter 1

FROM OPERA HAIR TO THE WORLD'S FAIR

Growing up in Lodz, Russia, Maksymilian Faktorowicz had the stuff Hollywood would be made of in his blood long before such a place was even conceived. As a boy, he dreamt of becoming a visual artist. His natural ability would eventually set him on the footpath to success. During his youth, Max worked a variety of jobs, including one where he sold fruit, peanuts and candy inside the lobby of the Czarina Theater in his hometown. The job gave him exposure to the performing arts—and "make-believe," as he would later tell a reporter—at a young age and would have a profound effect on that for which he would one day become a household name.

Extravagant wigs and makeup would come to define much of the fashion of Russian aristocracy during the 1800s. It was during this time that Max landed an apprenticeship with one of the most prominent wig makers in all of Lodz. Working his apprenticeship, young Max learned, practiced and ultimately perfected the art of wig making. Not long after, he would learn the craft of makeup application, practicing on local theater performers and models. He may have been inexperienced in comparison to some, but his natural talent spoke volumes, eventually landing him positions with other respected hair and makeup professionals. By the time he reached his early teens, he was offered a job with the prestigious Russian Grand Opera. Traveling throughout his country, he honed his skills on the most discriminating of opera divas, who appeared in the highest-caliber productions. His work would receive high-profile exposure, as the company often performed for Czar Nicholas and his family.

At the age of eighteen, Max Factor took a reprieve from his duties with the opera to serve an obligatory four-year stint in the military. Once his tour of duty ended, he returned to Russia and got right back on track, this time opening a costume shop in Moscow. He may have taken a sabbatical from makeup and wig artistry, but his talents didn't suffer. The young costumer's work with the opera had become so well known and respected that Max would receive an invitation to work for Czar Nicholas himself. Now, Max Factor was not only fashioning wigs and costumes for Russia's ruling class, but he was also making a pretty penny doing so.

But being at the beck and call of Russian aristocracy wasn't all it promised to be. An iron fist had long ruled the country, and Max's job was no different. His work was expected to be perfect to the point of ridiculousness, and although he often faced stress to the point of exhaustion, Max always delivered.

During his time working for the czar of Russia, Max met and married Esther Rosa. Though the young couple was very much in love, their happiness would be tainted by the ugly anti-Semitic attitudes and laws that prevailed in eighteenth-century Russia. Marriages between Poles and Jews were not only unaccepted but also illegal. Max and his young bride were forced to marry in secret and live separately.

Although he was uncertain of what the future held, Max knew if he stayed in his oppressive country, he would never live as a family with his wife and the three children—Freda, Cecilia and Davis—they now had. In 1904, with a sizeable bundle of cash he had saved (it's been said his nest egg totaled close to $40,000), Max and his family courageously boarded a steamship bound for America.

MEET ME IN ST. LOUIS

Near the turn of the century, St. Louis was growing into something of a bustling metropolis. Ornate Victorian mansions filled the city. Innovations such as electricity and the telephone were slowly replacing lanterns and telegraphs. The burgeoning railroad would serve as a modern substitute for the steamship as a choice of both travel and commerce. The booming iron and agricultural industries spurred economic and technological growth.

The presence of emancipated African Americans in St. Louis would influence the city's culinary and music styles. Texas-born ragtime pioneer Scott Joplin helped land the city on the music map, making it a hub for jazz. Immigrants from a variety of different countries would also come in large numbers to St. Louis, many first by way of Ellis Island, eventually connecting with family and, through courage and fortitude, forging out a brand-new existence in America. In 1904, St. Louis would become a world-class city when it hosted the grand dame of all events: the Louisiana Purchase Exposition. Also known as the World's Fair, the event would attract visitors by the thousands.

Exhibits ranging from visual and performing arts to inventions of the most unheard-of kinds dominated the magnificent Festival Hall. The lively music of a massive pipe organ boasting more than ten thousand pipes filled the air, restaurants that could seat up to 1,200 people at a time prepared mouth-watering dishes of all kinds of cuisines and a giant basin (called the Grand Basin) pumped forty-five thousand gallons of water through an enormous natural waterfall.

Hollywood had not even become a city when the cosmetician—now officially going by the more Americanized "Max Factor"—and his young family arrived in the United States. They landed first in New York and then made their way to St. Louis to join Max's uncle and brother. With the new business partner he had met on his journey, Max planned to open a booth at the giant exposition, selling his exquisite wigs, hairpieces and cosmetics, all of which had been highly sought after in his country. The cosmetics innovator was right at home with the entrepreneurial spirit that dominated the World's Fair of 1904. The two partners worked their booth with gusto, catering to customers and demonstrating their products. When the expo came to an end, their sales would prove they'd done a bustling business. Unfortunately, Max would learn his colleague had ulterior motives. When he went to retrieve his belongings from their exhibit booth, not only was the man nowhere to be found, but he'd also cleaned out the inventory and all of the money they'd made. Max had been swindled.

But the fleecing of Factor's cash and all of his goods wouldn't stop him; he knew he had other ways of making a living. With the help of his uncle and brother, Max opened a barbershop in downtown St. Louis. Located at 1513 Biddle Street, the business quickly gained a following for its wonderful services, which included haircuts, shampooing and a number of other refreshing treatments. Still, despite its success, barbering was not his true passion. What's more, in 1906, Factor would face major adversity when his beloved wife, Esther, died suddenly. Medical reports later confirmed that her death was caused by a brain hemorrhage. With nobody to help care for his children, the cosmetician wrote to family friends in Russia requesting the hand of their daughter in marriage. It was decided that the young woman would travel to St. Louis to join him. However, the union would be fraught with marital issues. And although Max's fourth child, son Louis, would be added to the brood, the couple's relationship would come to a nasty end. By the time he departed for Los Angeles, he had met and married his third wife, Jennie Cook, with whom he would stay until his passing in 1938. Despite the fact that his personal hardships had been many, he refused to let his circumstances stop him.

While working in his barbershop one day, he'd heard customers speaking—awestruck—about a brand-new pastime. Their enthusiasm surrounding motion pictures—or "photoplays," as they were called—made Factor want to experience one for himself. And once he did, it would be all the inspiration he needed.

Chapter 2

CINÉMOTOGRAPHE

What began in Fort Lee, New Jersey, during the late 1800s would grow into a star-studded industry, a movie-making mecca, with an entire region defined by its presence, instantly evoking images of glamour and fame at the mere mention of its name more than a century after being established.

When Max Factor arrived in Los Angeles in the autumn of 1908, the area that would eventually become Hollywood boasted more farmland and fruit trees than it did famous residents. The region had begun to experience a tremendous amount of growth. Land developer Henry Huntington would revolutionize tourism, launching the Huntington Hotel, as well as the city's "Red Car" system; maverick civil engineer William Mulholland transformed civil water access by engineering the Los Angeles aqueduct; and oil tycoon Burton E. Green laid the groundwork for what would become the city of Beverly Hills.

While moviemaking had already been underway in places such as New York, New Jersey and Philadelphia, in Southern California, there was no movie business to speak of. The Selig Polyscope Company would arrive around 1907, at the suggestion of producer and director Edwin Porter. During the filming of Porter's latest project, *The Count of Monte Cristo*, a discovery would be made, turning the tide—and the locales—of motion picture making for decades to come. Part of the film was supposed to be depicted in the Mediterranean. Fearing that audiences would recognize Central Park's already overused locations, Porter took his production west. He found the terrain versatile and the climate agreeable—so agreeable, in fact,

FILM PIONEER MACK SENNETT had been making a fortune cranking out silent films. One of the most popular actresses of the era, Mabel Normand (Normand was dubbed the "female Chaplin" for her comedic chops), had caught his eye. Although the two were involved professionally and romantically for years, that didn't stop Sennett's philandering with the many young starlets with whom he came in contact every day. It has been said that Sennett, looking for a way to appease his ladylove, built—at her demand—a state-of-the-art movie studio. The studio was the first completely enclosed soundstage of its kind, and like Selig Polyscope, Mack Sennett was located in Silver Lake. The name Edendale is long gone, but the tiny burg located adjacent to what would eventually become Hollywood remains a hub for writers and creatives—and it's still home to the now century-old Mack Sennett Studios.

that Selig Polyscope went back to California soon after it completed filming, this time building its own studio. Several years later, in 1912, Nestor Studio, the first full-scale independent studio, would be constructed in Edendale (the area known today as Silver Lake). Around the same time, Keystone Studios—later to be named Mack Sennett Studios—would be built, setting in place the establishment of many others to follow.

Near the turn of the century, the attractions for filmmakers to come west were many. With the medium of moviemaking still in its infancy, many of the sets and stages were constructed and shot outdoors, which required moderate weather temperatures for upward of twelve or more hours. This was something that could not be accomplished with the brutal, subzero temperatures of the east. And if winter wasn't an issue, heat and humidity were. Locations had become far too familiar to moviegoers, who in a short period of time had become quite sophisticated at deciphering backgrounds and locations where the scenes had been shot. Producers knew they must find an alternative to make their films credible. Some went to Cuba and others went to Florida, but most would find their way to California—permanently. Still, pastoral settings and good weather weren't the only reason they came.

Max Factor making up comedian Larry Semon in 1920, while actress Dorothy Dwan observes. Semon would write, direct and act in more than one hundred films during the silent era and gain immense popularity with his endearing expressions. He often appeared with his face painted stark white, a look for which he became famous.

Max Factor and actress Dorothy Phillips showing off one of the company's makeup kits in 1926. Although Phillips would appear in more than 150 films over the course of her career, her popularity would wane after 1927 with the advent of talkies—an all-too-common scenario for many silent film actors during this time.

THE LONG ARM OF THE TRUST

In 1908, Thomas Edison launched the Motion Picture Patents Corporation (MPPC). Edison, who owned nearly all of the patents having to do with motion picture cameras at that time, originally started the endeavor as a way to protect manufacturers and their mostly leased film equipment. In a short period of time, however, "the Trust," as it became known, quickly gained a monopoly over all of the major film companies, including Vitagraph, Biograph, American Pathé, Selig Polyscope and others. Trade patents became rigid and heavy handed, imposing restrictions on distribution, as well as on a film's length and running time, and a host of other regulations that had nothing to do with the leasing of camera equipment.

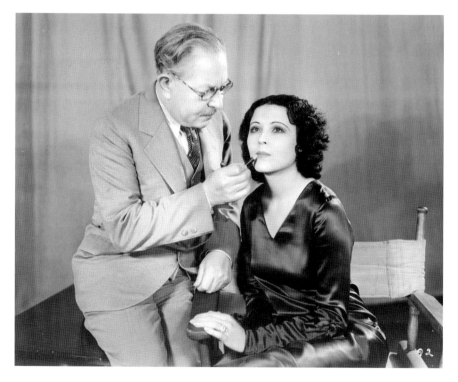

Max applying lipstick to Mexican American actress Raquel Torres. Despite the fact that Torres was of Mexican and German descent, the actress would play a variety of ethnicities, including a Polynesian beauty in the film *White Shadows of the South Seas* in 1928. The strikingly exotic Torres appeared in more than a dozen films throughout her career. This image appeared in the October 1930 issue of *Screenland* magazine, its original caption reading, "Making a beauty more beautiful—Max Factor, Hollywood make-up expert, helps Raquel Torres select the proper lipstick on set at the Metro-Goldwyn Mayer studios."

Max Factor tests makeup on the neck of French actress Renée Adorée in 1923. Born Jeanne de la Fontein into a family of circus performers (her father was a comic and her mother an equestrienne), Adorée would become one of the most popular actresses of the silent film era.

The harsh governing of the Trust would become too much for producers to bear. And although its ominous, imposing jurisdiction reached all the way to California, one thing was certain: it was far more difficult to know which companies were doing what when they were on the West Coast. Still, Edison employed many tactics in order to find out. On more than one occasion, he sent the Pinkerton Detective Agency to Los Angeles. Once there, agents would poke around in producers' business—even halting production for indefinite periods of time—to see if any violations had occurred. Ten years later, in 1918, to the relief of countless producers and other motion picture professionals, the Motion Picture Patents Corporation would permanently dissolve due to too many conflicts within the industry.

Opera singer Lawrence Tibbett and Catherine Dale Owen in the 1930 musical *The Rogue Song*.

Chapter 3
GREASEPAINT

In the early days of filmmaking, hours were long, sets were crude and conditions were less than stellar. Everything from lighting to makeup was done according to the theater, which had been the only form of production as far as the performing arts were concerned. Makeup for film simply did not exist in the early 1900s. When filmmaking made its way west after the turn of the century, actors, ever eager to land themselves a role, had begun using whatever they could find in order to create a feasible makeup solution for the camera. But their makeshift concoctions were lacking, to say the least. Materials, including everything from lard and Vaseline to brick dust, tobacco and cold cream, left much to be desired.

Max Factor may have been new to the city when he first got to Los Angeles in the autumn of 1908, but the cosmetician was not new to innovation. Soon after arriving, he opened Max Factor's Antiseptic Hair Store. The small shop was located at 1204 South Central Avenue and was in proximity to the city's many theaters. Moviemaking was a new medium, but with vaudeville in full swing, live theater was a bustling pastime for producers of traveling shows and actors who were looking to break into the brand-new movie business.

In his store, Factor sold various cosmetics he'd created, such as lip rouge and powder (though the goods wouldn't be specially packaged and sold as Max Factor and Company until later) and stocked his quality, custom-made wigs, toupees and goatees. Factor also carried the two most popular brands of theater greasepaint of the time: Leichner and Minor. But he was not satisfied selling someone else's products. He'd brought years of expertise to

Los Angeles with him and longed to branch out. Just as he'd done in Russia and St. Louis, Factor began to experiment with ingredients, making his own greasepaint for the theater, but despite its quality, it was a product that worked well for theater exclusively. Filmmaking was a different medium completely. In contrast to the one- or two-hour running time of a play, filming a movie took hours. Not only did theater greasepaint appear unflattering on film, but it also did not hold up long enough to make a motion picture. In addition to being thick and uncomfortable to wear, the substance cracked after being on the skin beyond a certain amount of time.

Hollywood Heritage Museum president Richard Adkins tells of the raw beginnings of filmmaking and makeup in the early days:

> *Motion pictures had slowly started coming west around 1907. There had been some innovations within the industry, but even by 1914, things were still very much done in terms of the theater as far as sets, costumes and makeup went. The kind of film they were using in those early days was orthochromatic, which was a very harsh, contrasting film. It had a tendency to make people appear very old, and so it was really unflattering for that reason because it aged the actor. Even an actor who was twenty years old would appear as if they were fifty years old with this kind of film and makeup combination.*
>
> *Another issue during this time was lighting. The stage lights that existed were mercury vapor lights. They were extremely hot and like orthochromatic film, they were tremendously unflattering to the actor. This type of lighting had worked in the theater but when it was used in filmmaking, did not flatter the appearance of the performers. As a result, they began to create their own greasepaint out of all kinds of materials because the theatrical makeup was just not suitable for film. It was very cakey and uncomfortable to wear on the skin, and it was ugly; and probably the worst thing about it was that it contained mercury and lead, which could cause illness and even be fatal. The contents were detrimental.*

GREASEPAINT REIGNS SUPREME

While the German-based Leichner and Minor brands of greasepaint had worked for the stage, nobody had come up with a product that was complimentary in appearance and safe enough to use. In 1914, Max Factor would create the first "flexible" greasepaint designed specifically for motion pictures. The brand-new product, which he dubbed Supreme Greasepaint, came in a range of twelve graduated shades, making it compatible with a variety of skin tones. The product was the first of its kind to be available in a tube—previously, theater makeup had been available only in a messy, unhygienic stick form—something that Factor had innovated, improving quality and sanitation. When applied to the skin, the product was flexible, creating a smooth, flawless finish, and unlike the one-size-fits-all makeup that had been used in theater for so long, Factor's supple, cream-based miracle product would not only hold up under the scorching lights and weather the long hours of filming but also enhance each and every face it was on. Some years later, Max Factor would journal about his earliest experiences developing Supreme Greasepaint for orthochromatic film:

[The] *first stars were Alice Joyce, Mabel Normand and Florence Lawrence. I used a bright yellow paint for their cheeks and dark greasepaint for their eyebrows. You may recall the terrifying FX's of the exaggerated*

Actress Mabel Normand with Max Factor at the Goldwyn Studio in 1920.

makeup on the screen. I experimented with the Gish sisters, Blanche Sweet, Louise Fazenda and four others. Gradually I developed a liquid makeup which was another milestone art of screen cosmetics.

In his book *Max Factor: The Man Who Changed the Faces of the World,* author Fred Basten tells how, in a short time, Max's store had become a revolving door of movie actors, as well as a social epicenter of sorts. John Barrymore, Charlie Chaplin, Marie Dressler and a slew of other future screen legends would come into the shop to have their faces made up by Max or just to say hello. Supreme Greasepaint was so well liked and sought after that it would even turn super macho cowboy actor Tom Mix into a fan. It was widely known that Mix prided himself on steering clear of makeup products, calling them all "too sissy." However, once he'd seen how much Max's new paint could enhance his already strong features for the better, Mix became a believer, too, further adding to Factor's growing legion of fans around town. And that isn't all. Max's quality products and makeup techniques were in such demand that he started opening his shop earlier and earlier in order to accommodate the actors who needed to be made up at an hour that would allow them to make their call times. Some actors had even begun requesting that Max travel to the film's location to do their makeup on set. And once he did, he would become more in demand than ever.

COLOR HARMONY

Max Factor created Supreme Greasepaint in 1914, to the delight of actors and producers all over town. In February 1917, Paramount Pictures released the feature film *Joan the Woman,* which starred Geraldine Farrar. By this time, the cosmetics guru had beautified scads of silent movie stars. The 1917 film would be the first picture up until that point for which anyone had ever analyzed and consulted with the issues of filming and lighting exclusively in terms of makeup. Max Factor would direct the entire process from start to finish, systematically choosing makeup and hair looks for each scene before the production even started, further expanding his professional repertoire and expertise.

His growing popularity would only fuel his desire to create even more revolutionary products. Factor was constantly looking for ways to enhance the natural beauty of the actors he worked with, using only the highest-quality ingredients. In 1918, he launched the Color Harmony principle

An advertisement for Color Harmony Makeup featuring Carole Lombard. This ad appeared in *Screenland* magazine in 1934 and was publicity for Max Factor makeup, as well as for Lombard's latest movie, *Bolero*.

AT STUDIO...

DINNER DANCE...

or BEACH

"Born to be Kissed"
M-G-M Production starring
Jean Harlow
with
Franchot Tone

Jean HARLOW'S *Beauty* Is Always Fascinating

JEAN HARLOW'S
COLOR
HARMONY
MAKE-UP

...Max Factor's
Flesh Face Pow-
der to blend with
her fair skin.

...Max Factor's
Flame Rouge to
give a touch of har-
monizing color.

...Max Factor's
Super-Indelible
Flame Lipstick to
accent the lips.

Would YOU Like to Share Her MAKE-UP SECRET?

IN Hollywood, a genius created a new kind of make-up for the screen stars ... and now for you. It is color harmony make-up, originated by Max Factor.

POWDER ... *You will note the difference in the caressing smoothness. You will see a satin-smooth effect like the beauty you see flashed on the screen. You will marvel how naturally the color harmony enlivens the beauty of your skin. Max Factor's Face Powder, one dollar.* **ROUGE** ... *You will see how beautifully a color tone in rouge can harmonize with your powder and complexion colorings. As you blend your rouge coloring, you'll note how soft and fine it is, like the most delicate skin-texture. Max Factor's Rouge, fifty cents.* **LIPSTICK** ... *Super-Indelible, for lipstick must be lasting in Hollywood, and you, too, will find it permanent and uniform in color. It is moisture-proof, too ... so that you may be sure of a perfect lip make-up that will last for hours. Max Factor's Super-Indelible Lipstick, one dollar.*

Max Factor ★ Hollywood

SOCIETY MAKE-UP
Face Powder, Rouge and Lipstick in COLOR HARMONY

A 1932 promotion for Max Factor makeup and Jean Harlow's latest film, *Born to Be Kissed,* a title that would later be changed to *The Girl from Missouri.*

of makeup. In his research, Factor had discovered that certain combinations of hair color and each woman's varying complexion required a particular palette of makeup colors. Additionally, Factor discerned that certain makeup shades and colors naturally complemented certain hair and eye colors and skin complexions; it had become evident that one-size-fits-all makeup was not an option. He knew that it was all about customizing an array of colors for the many contrasting combinations.

> "Only actresses and harlots would have been seen in it—not respectable women."
> —Max Factor

With this new discovery, a major hurdle within makeup had been overcome. Max could now match each actor's face—whether male or female—with the correct shade of makeup, be it rouge, powder or his glorious Supreme Greasepaint. This was a huge development for Factor, as it would later serve as the basis for Society MakeUp. Even better, because wearing makeup was still a long way from being commonplace (aside from the theater performer and the movie star), everyday women who lacked the know-how to properly apply makeup would eventually use the practical principles to choose the correct shades and tones that harmonized with their unique combination of features. The Color Harmony principle would be a foolproof way for women everywhere to achieve a look that was perfect for them.

Some years later, when Factor took Jean Harlow's lackluster locks from a drab shade of dishwater to a shocking shade of blond he named "platinum," not only did the look catapult Harlow to superstardom, but it also started a national color trend that would last for more than five years. But although Harlow's hair color was a groundbreaking success, it would present a particular problem. The stark platinum blond color against her fair skin forced Factor to create another category within Color Harmony to suit Harlow's distinctive hair and complexion dilemma. Like he had done with so many other faces, Factor solved the issue by creating a category for women who possessed Harlow's same hair, eye and skin color combination. The Color Harmony principle first created by Max Factor had such an impact that it would lay the groundwork for a system that is still used by makeup artists and cosmetics manufacturers to this day.

BEAUTY MAY BE DOUBLED

Do you apply your powder first, or your rouge first? For soft, beautiful coloring, rouge first... always. The powder profusely, removing the surplus with Face Powder Brush. And remember when you select your Powder, Rouge, and Super-Indelible Lipstick... consider your personality as well as your complexion! Are you vivacious? Are you demure? Among the nine life-like shades in Powder, seven in Rouge and the four Color Harmony tones in Super-Indelible Lipstick, you will find the ideal combination to double your beauty.

THERE IS ART IN MAKE-UP

And if you will become acquainted with a few professional rules of make-up, you will realize there is an art, too, in a puff of powder and a pat of rouge. To give your cheeks the smoothness of velvet, and to make your powder and rouge adhere perfectly, start your make-up with powder foundation.

From a 1930s Color Harmony product booklet

COLOR HARMONY

Make-Up Easy... If You Learn These Secrets

To accomplish this effect is easy if you know what constitutes make-up; if you learn the correct method of make-up; and if you select the correct color harmony to blend with your natural complexion.

First, then, make-up requires that each feature, which adds to beauty, must be considered individually and as a part of the harmonious whole. The face, the eyes, the lips, the neck, the arms, the hands, the hair—each should be beautified.

Second, make-up should not be used in a haphazard fashion, but should be applied according to certain well-defined principles of art and cosmetic science.

Third, all cosmetics used must be in perfect color harmony with the individual complexion, or else they clash, producing an unnatural, grotesque effect.

From a 1930s Color Harmony advertisement

Actress Marjorie Weaver applying lip rouge with a makeup brush in 1936.

Demonstrating the proper application of facial powder for a 1937 publicity photo.

Tube mascara, first introduced by Max Factor Jr., would not emerge until the 1950s. In this 1930s photo, the elder Factor applies eyelash mascara from a cake to an unknown model. The precision of his technique can be seen as he uses his index finger to gently pull the lash upward in order to achieve a dramatic effect.

Chapter 4

A BRAND-NEW NAME

Makeup was neither a new idea nor a new term by 1920. Theater and vaudeville performers had been using it to describe the stuff they applied to their faces before taking the stage for decades, but in civilized society, the word had been associated with all things unsavory. Thankfully, none of these sentiments stopped Max Factor. Since his arrival in Los Angeles more than a decade earlier, he'd been on a roll engineering the next greatest beauty item. He invented the hair color—and coined the term—"brownette." Not only were Judy Garland and Rochelle Hudson proud wearers of the color, but the intoxicating shade of sable with a reddish tint also made up the hair color of nearly 50 percent of all women.

In 1916, Factor introduced the eyebrow pencil and eye shadow within Society MakeUp, the line he created exclusively for the stars that would later be available to the public. By 1917, ever ahead of his time, he had invented a tool that would become a precursor to a beauty staple for women even today: MakeUp Blender. Designed first for stage performers and introduced later to motion picture actors and eventually the general public, Factor's MakeUp Blender was created to apply makeup to the neck, forearms and shoulders—everywhere the facial makeup line ended—to achieve continuity and a glamorizing effect, the naked eye unable to detect where the skin ends and the makeup begins.

Max Factor's revolutionary cosmetics had become a smashing success within the theater and motion picture communities. They were catching on with high-society women and the wives of dignitaries and movie producers and now were taking the female public by storm. Still referring to his high-quality beautification items as "cosmetics," Max would take a chance at the suggestion of his son Frank in 1920. The younger Factor was aware that makeup had been a term associated with the uncouth. At the same time, his father had made such strides. Their business was booming. They catered to the leading ladies and leading men of Hollywood. They'd launched makeup trends and created custom looks for the stars that regular women had begun to emulate. Frank Factor felt his father's innovations had been so unprecedented that the public could do nothing but embrace them all the way. In 1920, Max Factor would acquiesce, taking his son's advice and officially calling his products "makeup" publicly from that point forward. The enticing new word used to describe their beauty wares had zing and selling appeal—and more and more, women everywhere couldn't wait to get their hands on them.

Actress Mae Murray puckers up for Max Factor in 1928. Murray began her move through the ranks of show business first as a chorus girl in the *Ziegfeld Follies* and later as an actress in silent films. She would make her film debut in the adventure drama *To Have and to Hold* in 1916. Her irresistible combination of coyness and coquette—along with some makeup magic from Max Factor—earned her the nickname "the girl with the bee-stung lips."

USEFUL GLAMOUR HINTS AND MAKE-UP TRICKS

IN APPLYING MAKE-UP allow enough time to do it well and make sure your light is good. During the day, work by daylight in front of a window if possible. At night, an illuminated make-up mirror provides excellent light.

KEEP SKIN FRESHENER AND COLOGNE in your refrigerator, or a cool place. Chilled, it can be as bracing as a trip to the mountains.

IF YOU WEAR GLASSES, don't wear exaggerated bangs. Sweep your hair to one side, revealing your full brow. Choose earrings in proper proportion to your glasses and make sure glasses are the right size and shape for your face. Avoid bright coloured eyeshadow; wear brown or grey. Use eyelash make-up, but in moderation, with a minimum amount on your lower lashes. Emphasize the arch of your eyebrows as much as possible, but still keep them natural looking. Don't apply too much rouge, as any lens magnification will make it appear too obvious. Be certain the frames of your glasses do not clash in colour with the shades of your lipstick and rouge.

CLOSE-SET EYES can be made to appear wider apart by increasing distance between eyebrows with tweezers.

HOLLOW CHEEKS should have rouge blended above the hollows, not in them. Since rouge serves as a shadow, this application neutralizes the natural shadows in the hollows, making cheeks appear fuller and attractively rounding the contour of the face.

IF YOUR NOSE IS LONG, apply foundation make-up in a darker shade, than you use on your face than to the under tip of your nose. Blend the edges with your fingertips to avoid any lines of demarcation.

THE BRIDGE OF YOUR NOSE can be made to appear more prominent, if too flat, by applying Eye Shadow on the upper lids towards nose and penciling eyebrows closer together.

IF YOUR EARS ARE LARGE, apply foundation make-up to the ears in a darker shade than you use on your face. This will make them appear less conspicuous. Wear large earrings that clamp over your ear lobes and cover them. Avoid small or drop earrings.

WHEN YOU POSE FOR A BLACK-AND-WHITE PORTRAIT wear a clear red shade of lipstick. Light pinks, corals, orange reds and fuchsias will not photograph well. Do not wear rouge unless it is a light shade. A dark shade will photograph as a shadow and might distort the shape of your face. Wear your hair in the simplest, most becoming style.

A SHEEN TO FINISH YOUR FACE can be achieved after your make-up has been completely applied by patting on Skin Freshener or Astringent with a damp sponge and allowing it to dry naturally.

*From the 1954 Max Factor and Company product booklet You at Your Lovliest

"Greta Garbo, Marlene Dietrich and others would often stop into Schwab's Pharmacy on Sunset Boulevard to pick up their favorite mascara and lipstick. In those days, Schwab's carried Max Factor."
—Marc Wanamaker

Chapter 5

MAKEUP GOES MAINSTREAM

Walk through the cosmetics area of any department store today and you'll see a virtual beauty blitz—from free makeovers and giveaways to gifts-with-purchase, food, drinks, DJs and live music—all to announce the launch of a brand's latest product. Cosmetics companies stop at nothing to boost their sales and build a loyal following. This is not a new idea by modern standards, but in the 1920s, going to such lengths was virtually unheard of. The ever-innovative Max Factor would blaze new trails, not just within cosmetics and the public's embracing of them, but with publicizing them as well.

With the help of his sons and small staff, Factor had been hard at work turning some of Hollywood's most beautiful young ingénues into major stars. The idea of everyday women wearing makeup was slowly gaining acceptance. Moviegoing had become one of the country's favorite pastimes. Week after week, young women all across the country would go to picture shows and admire the beauty Factor was bringing to the screen.

He had been successful at manufacturing the highest-quality products anywhere around, inventing tooth-whitening enamel (a precursor to the hundreds of whitening products available today), powder blush and false eyelashes (Phyllis Haver would be the first actress ever to don a set of false lashes, custom made for her by Max Factor), and he even concocted a not-so-glamorous (but effective, nonetheless) shampoo to treat head lice aptly named "Kill 'Em Quick," which often showed itself on the transitory film sets of the early days. His products had become so popular with the stars who wore them

During the 1920s, Max Factor brought cosmetics to the masses with a series of public makeup demonstrations. The well-received events were held everywhere from movie theater lobbies to department stores. This poster reflects one of the events—including its prizes—at the Venice Ballroom.

A poster for one of Max Factor and Company's makeup contests held at the Venice Beach Pier. The super popular events would see young women by the hundreds, all hoping to win a bevy of Max Factor beauty products or, even better, a chance to screen test for a Hollywood producer.

that moviegoers saw them and wanted the look for themselves. His celebrity clients were truly fans of his cosmetics and were more than happy to endorse them—even for the meager one-dollar paycheck they received for doing so; it didn't matter, to demonstrate Max Factor cosmetics in an advertisement was a privilege. Max had won the respect of nearly every actor in Hollywood.

Factor's eldest sons had helped their father run his store since the family arrived in Los Angeles. It was known that while Davis Factor had a mind for business, Frank was gifted at the innovation of perfumes and cosmetics. The three Factor men would take marketing to a new level by hosting a series of makeup demonstrations and contests all around Los Angeles. Everywhere from movie house lobbies to drugstores and department stores—even the Venice Beach Pier—were popular venues to hold the exhibitions, and they always drew a vast crowd. Colorful posters could be seen all over town advertising the next upcoming contest. Not only could young women find out how to make the most of their natural beauty by learning to correctly apply Max Factor's superb cosmetics, but they could also walk away looking like movie stars—or even better, one lucky winner could be the recipient of a gift basket filled with Society MakeUp or a real screen test and a shot at making it in the big time. The events were a giant success, but Max's main concern remained one thing: to show every young woman in attendance how to correctly apply makeup. One by one, women were transformed by utilizing the tips and techniques Factor taught them. Eventually, the demonstrations became so popular that Max would employ trained assistants to do the demonstrations, but by that time, the products had more than caught on with the general public. Max Factor had become a household name.

Goodbye Orthochromatic

"Greasepaint dropping out as cosmetic," "greasepaint is abandoned" and "greasepaint to be taboo" were only some of the sensational headlines making front-page news by the end of the 1920s, a time that would bring much change within motion pictures. Previously unknown faces of the silver screen had become bona fide matinee idols; organizations such as the American Society of Motion Pictures and the Motion Picture Makeup Association had begun cropping up around town, putting in place new standards within the industry. The advent of synchronized sound with the 1927 film *The Jazz Singer* signified the end of the silent picture era, a transition that brought with it a host of technical issues. The jump from the blue-sensitive orthochromatic film to the use of full color–range panchromatic called for new lighting and makeup solutions.

Despite Factor's groundbreaking formulation with Supreme Greasepaint some ten years earlier, technology was changing. Factor's greasepaint, which had once worked wonders, now clashed with panchromatic film. Stars who had loved the once-indispensable makeup were faced with the prospect of having to appear on screen looking like something from a horror film or, even worse, appear with a naked face before the camera. A 1920s newspaper article from the personal scrapbook of Cecil B. DeMille, describes the changing industry standards and sentiments of the time:

Since the beginning of the motion picture industry, greasepaint, in a multitude of forms, has ruled the screen. Now suffering film folk and also suffering film fans are seeing its overthrow. Improved cameras, better lighting and more sensitive film are making it possible for the star to appear before the lens without reinforced layers of grease and cosmetics. In early days, faces were done in yellow to make them photograph lighter. Since then they have passed through most of the colors of the rainbow, with some actors even using blue and purple paints to gain a better effect. Women with their finer skin and lighter coloring faired well enough but the "he-men" of the thrillers were wont to be reflected with faces of "ghastly pallor" but with necks and arms that photograph as shocking challenge to soap and water. But even with the technical improvements made dethroning of King Grease Paint is not without a struggle. Actors recruited from the stage are hard to wean from the grease pot. They blush at the facial nudity of acting a part without a mask of paint. The announcement that Cecil B. DeMille [made] *that he will produce his next picture without grease paint being used by any of the players stirred some protest, more of it, surprisingly, from the men than from the women. Allan Dwan is directing the Paramount Picture, "Sea Horses"* [and] *had a cast including Florence Vidor, Jack Holt, William Powell, George Bancroft and others that used no make-up and it was successful. Other film folk who have dropped the use of makeup for the screen include Esther Ralston, Mary Brian, Betty Bronson, Theodore Roberts, Wallace Berry, Jane Novak, Ernest Torrence, Raymond Hatton and Alice Terry.*

The onset of the makeup upheaval prompted Max to get busy experimenting on a more viable option that would complement the complexion of the

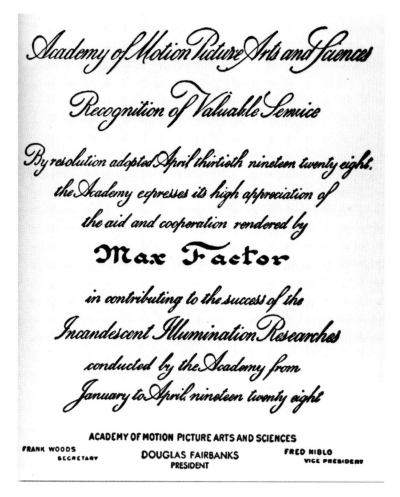

Academy of Motion Picture Arts and Sciences

Recognition of Valuable Service

By resolution adopted April thirtieth nineteen twenty eight, the Academy expresses its high appreciation of the aid and cooperation rendered by

Max Factor

in contributing to the success of the Incandescent Illumination Researches conducted by the Academy from January to April nineteen twenty eight

ACADEMY OF MOTION PICTURE ARTS AND SCIENCES

FRANK WOODS
SECRETARY

DOUGLAS FAIRBANKS
PRESIDENT

FRED NIBLO
VICE PRESIDENT

When film made the jump from orthochromatic to panchromatic, Max Factor would engineer a formula that was compatible with the color-sensitive film. Upon its completion in 1928, the Academy of Motion Picture Arts and Sciences presented him with an award.

actors and work well with panchromatic film. In addition to considering matters of color (unlike orthochromatic, panchromatic film was sensitive to a full color range within black-and-white film), Max was aware of the psychological effects that going before the camera sans makeup could have on his actors, whose very livelihoods hinged on how flawless their faces appeared. Factor joined forces with the motion picture studios. Together they worked to develop a formula that was compatible across the board. After nearly two years of experimentation, Factor would emerge

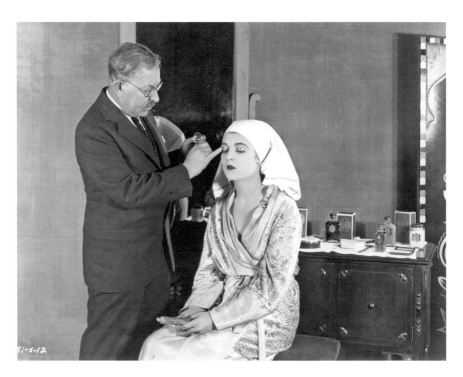

Actress Dorothy Dwan with her eyes closed and hair smoothed back under a pristine white towel as Max Factor delicately applies iridescent shadow to her eyelid. In her hand, Dwan holds a tube of Supreme Greasepaint. One can get a clear idea of the flawlessness achieved by Factor's expertise in this photo, as evidenced by the stunning makeup job.

with Panchromatic Makeup. Thinner than Supreme Greasepaint, more natural to the touch and easy to apply, Panchromatic Makeup (still largely referred to as "greasepaint") worked wonders in solving technical issues where color was concerned and made stars' complexions appear even more perfect on screen than they previously had. And unlike Supreme, Panchromatic contained powder to reduce shine and, thus, reflection on camera.

Max Factor had created a formula so relevant that it would set the industry standard from that point forward, becoming the makeup against which all motion picture studios would measure their products. And nearly every movie studio in the United States and Europe would stock the shelves of their makeup departments with it. In 1929, Max Factor was presented with a certificate from the Academy of Motion Pictures Arts and Sciences for his groundbreaking development of the new cosmetic.

MAKE-UP IS A DOZEN times more important to-day than it ever was. Three years ago the players were beautiful or handsome of feature, and got their jobs because of that. Some greasepaint, powder, lip-rouge and an eye pencil were enough make-up. Then the talkies came. The pretty boys and girls stammered, squeaked, and—experienced stage folk came along to take their places. They weren't always beautiful—for instance, the dyed-in-the-business character people, and we had to beautify them, men and women. Others were beautiful, particularly as to coloring, for on the stage color harmony counted more than features. When color was added to pictures, it helped the stage players more than the picture people, but we had to start all over again with an entirely new type of make-up.

Max Factor on the evolution of motion picture makeup in a 1930 interview

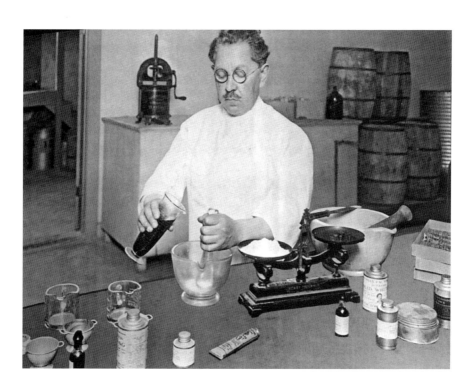

HOW TO APPLY MAX FACTOR'S PANCHROMATIC MAKE-UP

Preparing the Face—The face must be thoroughly cleaned before make-up is applied. The best way is to wash the face with soap and water. Men should be smoothly shaven.

Base for Grease Paint—It is often necessary to use cold cream before applying grease paint. In my laboratory, however, we have developed a grease paint, which eliminates this need.

Grease Paint Application—Squeeze about one-quarter of an inch of grease paint from the tube into the palm of the hand. Then with the tips of the fingers of the other hand apply the grease paint in "dibs and dabs," covering the face with little dots of grease paint until it acquires the appearance of a freckled face. Grease paint must be applied sparingly, too much will spoil your make-up.

Spreading Grease Paint—Now remove the grease paint from the hands and dip them into cool water, then with the finger tips moistened with water spread the grease paint over the face, blending it smoothly, evenly and thinly into the skin. The movement of the fingers should be from the center of the face outward. Keep dipping fingertips into water, as it is essential to blend the grease paint in order to have a smooth and thin application.

*A 1930 product brochure for Panchromatic Makeup

Opposite: A photo of Max Factor that appeared in the July 1934 issue of *Hollywood Filmograph* magazine. The original caption read, "The dean and daddy of all cosmeticians is Max Factor, who is pictured above in his laboratory at the Max Factor Make-Up Studios. According to facts and figures that make up cinema history, Max Factor gave us the first make-up to give natural tones to the skin in 1920; the first perspiration-proof liquid body make-up in 1923; the first under-water make-up in 1926; the perfection of Panchromatic make-up in 1928; the first Sunburn-Waterproof make-up in 1929; and Satin Smooth make-up in 1934. What a background of achievement! It is indeed a mighty parade of progress, and worthy of a place in the cinema hall of fame."

Max Factor and actress Silvia Sidney, whose expressive features and unique look earned her two distinct monikers: "The woman with the saddest eyes in Hollywood" and "The woman with the heart-shaped face." Here, Sidney applies eyelash mascara at the Max Factor Makeup Studio in Hollywood, 1934.

Chapter 6

SOCIETY MAKEUP

B y 1920, Hollywood had been following Max Factor for more than a decade. Catering to the brightest stars in the business, Max had become personal makeup artist and hair stylist—sometimes even confidant and counselor—for nearly every big name in Tinsel Town (Rudolph Valentino, Joan Crawford and Mary Pickford among them). He'd gained a strong following within high-society circles with wives of dignitaries, producers and politicians, all of whom were clamoring to try the transformational cosmetics for themselves. Building on his immensely popular Color Harmony technique, the cosmetics wizard would launch another beauty bombshell: Society MakeUp. Knowing how vulgar the word "makeup" had been regarded in the not-so-distant past, he knew the word "society" would give the cosmetics more clout and credibility than ever before. As he'd done many times, Factor used the most glamorous guinea pigs around—his actresses—to test his new cosmetics. From rouge and lipstick to greasepaint and eyebrow pencil, Factor knew one thing: if actresses took a liking to it, he would have it produced, packaged and released to the public. Stars not only loved his products, but they also endorsed them in magazines, newspapers and the like—and with good reason. The packaging was irresistible, the actresses were drop-dead gorgeous and the ads almost always coincided with the release of their latest pictures.

MAKEUP FOR EVERYBODY

Everyday women could now wear makeup proudly, making a statement of their individual beauty and, at the same time, emulating the looks of their favorite movie stars. Colorful print magazines such as *Screenland*, *Motion Picture* and others, featuring celebrities, domestic tips and the latest fashion trends, had become popular. Along with advertisements for Max Factor Makeup, order forms were included. Women everywhere could now order for themselves—straight from Hollywood to their front doorsteps—the very makeup worn by Loretta Young, Carole Lombard and other screen goddesses. Factor's products contained the highest-quality ingredients, and what's more, they delivered what they promised: to enhance the looks of every single woman who wore them by bringing out her natural beauty. Society MakeUp was sold throughout the United States and London, making it the first international makeup available to the public worldwide.

THE NEW ART OF SOCIETY MAKEUP

Leaving no stone unturned when it came to educating women on the correct application of makeup, Max Factor and Company included pamphlets with detailed instructions in their packaging. In addition, brochures often accompanied Max Factor product displays and could be found on makeup counters at the famed Hollywood showroom, as well as at drug and sundries stores such as Schwab's, which was known for having stocked Max Factor makeup. To the delight of the female consumer, stars such as Bette Davis, Claudette Colbert, Ginger Rogers and others were regularly featured in Society MakeUp booklets. The lofty advertisements piqued the imaginations of women everywhere, allowing them to envision themselves looking ever so stunning opposite Errol Flynn or Gary Cooper.

In addition to the legions of actresses who loved Max Factor, wives of dignitaries and society women were also among some of his most devoted fans. Here, Factor applies powder to the face of a Miss Jones in 1937.

"DREAM A MOMENT... THEN fly on the wings of imagination to Hollywood. ...It is night-time at one of the big studios. ...A Rolls-Royce silently and gracefully rolls up to the entrance. ...The star alights and hurries to her dressing room. ...At her make-up table Max Factor is interestedly working. ...There is something new tonight. ...The genius in make-up has developed another discovery...tonight color pigments will be harmonized in cosmetics for the first time. ...As the star is being made up she wonders if the experiment will be a success. ...The camera will tell, for the camera never lies. ...On the set, under the 'Klieg' lights, the director marvels at her radiant beauty. ...Max Factor enthusiastically smiles approval. ...Intuitively she senses a success as the camera starts clicking. ...Now, later...the review of the film in the projection room...and as the scene flashes on the screen, the rare beauty of the star appears so lovely, so natural, so alluring, that Max Factor realizes the severe test of the Klieg lights has caused him to develop a revolutionary idea in cosmetics. Thus, the science of cosmetic color harmony was discovered."

*The New Art of Society MakeUp advertisement, circa 1920s

HOW TO APPLY LIPSTICK

1

DRY the lips. Lipstick will adhere properly only to a dry lip. Make up the upper lip first. With lipstick follow the contour of the lip and fill in by blending with lipstick or the finger.

2

TRACE this lip contour on the lower lip by simply compressing the lips together. This transfers the color pattern from the upper lip to the lower lip and assures a symmetrical attractive mouth.

3

FILL in and blend the lipstick on the lower lip and smooth lipstick on the upper lip. Rub well towards inside of mouth to eliminate *lipstick line*. Now moisten lips to give them luster and allure.

4

THE colour of your lipstick should harmonise with the color of your rouge and powder. Use Max Factor's Super-Indelible Lipstick in the correct shade. Your lip make-up will remain perfect all day, smooth in texture and permanent in colour and value.

HOW TO APPLY EYE MAKE-UP

1

APPLY Max Factor's Eye Shadow lightly to the upper lid only. Blend lightly, ever so delicately—creating a smooth even colour-tine from the eyelash to the eyebrow.

2

WITH Max Factor's Eyebrow Pencil to outline and define and shape of the eyebrows, follow the natural curve of the eyebrow to the end of the brow, extending the line a trifle.

3

USE Max Factor's Eyebrow Pencil to outline and define the eye. Where the eyelash meets the lower lid, draw a fine line, forming a faint shadow back of the lashes. Do not overdo this so that it becomes obvious.

4

APPLY Max Factor's Masque or Eyelash Make-Up to the upper lashes first. Apply with an upward stroke to the upper lashes; with a downward stroke to the lower lashes. Then separate lashes with a small brush.

HOW TO APPLY FACE POWDER

1

START powdering at the lower cheeks. Gently pat and blend powder toward centre of face. Powder the nose last; otherwise the nose will be over-powdered, making it appear conspicuous.

2

NOW with the powder lightly into the tiny lines around the eyes, nose, mouth and chin. This assures a completely powdered surface.

3

WITH the Max Factor Face Powder Brush, lightly brush away surplus powder, clearing all lines at the eyes, nose, mouth and chin, giving your make-up a velvety, even finish.

4

THUS, with Max Factor's Face Powder in the correct colour harmony shade is created a stain-smooth make-up that clings for hours... colour perfect and flattering under any light.

HOW TO APPLY ROUGE

1

APPLY Max Factor's Rouge with the puff. Pat, do not rub. Start your rouge at the high point of the cheek and follow the natural curve of the cheekbone towards the nose. The colour should trace a slight curve.

2

WITH the fingers, blend the rouge into the full parts of the cheek; soften the edges of the colour pattern by blending; and blend again so that the colour seems to suffuse the cheeks.

3

CARRY the rouge very faintly from the cheekbones to the outer corner of the lower eyelid. This eliminates the white space between the cheekbone and the eye, and adds naturalness to rouging.

4

ROUGE should appear natural, not obvious. Choose your correct colour harmony shade in Max Factor's Rouge... its perfect colour, its delicate texture and creamy smoothness aid in faultless, lasting make-up.

SPECIAL INSTRUCTIONS FOR EVENING

In the evening at social functions, dances, and in cafés, you will find that your natural daytime make-up will be toned down by the artificial light. Therefore I recommend a more enlivening color harmony for each type.

*Directions for applying Max Factor and Company's Society MakeUp

PRICE LIST

FACE POWDER, $1.00
White, Flesh, Rachelle, Natural,
Olive,
Brunette, Ochre, Sum'r Tan,
Evening.

FACE POWDER BRUSH, $1.00

ROUGE, .50
Nos. 12, 18, 24, Blondeen,
Flame,
Carmine, Raspberry, Natural,
Day.

SUPER-INDELIBLE LIPSTICK, $1.00
Flame, Vermillion, Carmine,
Crimson.

LIPSTICK, .50
Light, Medium, Dark.

LIP POMADE, .50
Light, Medium, Dark.

EYE SHADOW, .50
Brown, Gray, Blue, Green

EYEBROW PENCIL, .50
Black, Brown.

EYEBROW PENCIL - Purse-size, .50
Black, Brown.

MASQUE, .50
Black, Brown.

EYELASH MAKE-UP, $1.00
Mascara in Black, Brown and Blue.

DOUBLE VANITY, $1.50
Loose powder style, with rouge.

ROUGE REFILLS, .25
Nos. 18, 24, Blondeen,
Raspberry,
Natural.

POWDER FOUNDATION, $1.00
White, Flesh, Rachelle, Natural.

HONEYSUCKLE CREAM, $1.00
Extra-large professional size,
$2.00

SKIN FRESHENER, $1.00

ASTRINGENT, $1.00
Extra-large professional size,
$2.00

CLEASNING CREAM, $1.00
Cream or Liquid.
Extra-large professional size,
$2.00

MELTING CLEANSING CREAM,
$1.00

LEMON CREAM, $1.00
Solid or Liquid.

SKIN AND TISSUE CREAM, $1.00
Extra-large professional size,
$2.00

BLEACH MASK, $1.00
Extra-large professional size,
$2.00

MAKE-UP BLENDER, $1.00
White, Flesh, Rachelle, Natural.

EAU DE COLOGNE, $1.00

BRILLOX, .50 and $1.00

MANICURE MAKE-UP:
Liquid Nail Polish, Nail Tint,
Cuticle
Remover, Cuticle Cream, Nail
Polish,
Nail White—each .50
Nail Enamel Remover, .25

M A X   F A C T O R
M A K E - U P
H O L L Y W O O D

Society MakeUp product and price list

YOUR MAKE-UP PROBLEMS

Dear Mr. Factor:—I am sixteen and my parents object to my wearing make-up. I know several girls of my age who use make-up and really you would hardly know it. I am sure if you will tell me how to do it, my parents will not object when they see how much it improves me—I am a medium brunette, brown hair—dark eyes, which sometimes look almost hazel, and my skin is not fair. Appreciating yours,

Maude S.,
Dayton, Ohio

Answer:—It is my suggestion if you wish to win approval of your parents, that you use make-up very sparingly. Before purchasing any make-up find out the condition of your skin—whether dry or oily, so that you may be able to get the preparations best suited, as make-up must be durable and natural, otherwise it defeats its own purpose. The proper shades for your type are: Natural powder, Medium Lip Rouge and Raspberry Dry Rouge.

Dear Mr. Factor:—I am giving a play for my church and there are three characters in it. I play the heavy—A man about thirty. A boy of eighteen with dark eyes and hair plays the hero, while the heroin, for contrast, is a blonde. My own make-up and the hero's I can manage quite well, thanks to your previous suggestions, but while I know the girl's general type, I am puzzled on how to make up her eyes—they bulge—really it is a pity, as otherwise she would be very pretty. Will you please advise me how to overcome this defect? Thanking you for your many past courtesies, I am.

Sincerely yours,
Charles McA.,
St. Paul, Minn.

Answer: Bulging eyes are successfully concealed by shadowing the upper lid with a dark purple lining color and high-lighting the center with a contrasting shade of the lining color. The highlight is applied over the shadow in the center of the lids. For the lower lid, draw a line as close as you can to the lash line with an eyebrow pencil and smudge it well into the complexion, blending the edges of the line, which gives a dark shadow, setting the eyes back.

Dear Mr. Factor:—There has always been a doubt in my mind on the correct way of applying eyeshadow. I am a brunette. What shade should I wear, and is it appropriate for daytime. Thanking you very kindly for your reply, I am,

L.B.,
Redondo Beach, Calif.

Answer:—Apply a thin film of Eyeshadow to the eyelids with your fingertips, using a light outward motion, blending it carefully upward and outward toward the eyebrows and the outer edges of the lids. No decided line should be visible. For a brunette, a soft shade of brown should be used. It is appropriate for day and eveningwear.

Dear Mr. Factor:—I have a receding chin, otherwise the contour of my face is not so bad. Will you please tell me how I can overcome this defect. I know how you use your wonderful Make-up already, already having "found my type," so to speak.

Sincerely yours,
Grace B.,
Mount Vernon, N.Y.

Answer:—To offset this effect it is necessary to use a powder blended into the chin that you use on the other parts of your face. In that manner your chin will appear more prominent by being of a lighter shade than your general complexion.

Dear Mr. Factor:—I have read about the wonderful evening make-up worn by the various screen stars and social celebrities at the Previews. Will you tell me how to accomplish the same effect. I am a natural blonde—my parents are from Norway—with blue eyes and very white skin.

Thelma G.,
Fresno, Calif.

Answer:—A perfect Blonde with your complexion should wear flesh powder, Bright lipstick, Blondeen Dry Rouge, blue eyeshadow, and touch up the eyebrows with a brown pencil and brown masque for coloring the lashes.

Dear Mr. Factor:—As a result of scalding water falling on my face when I was a baby, I have a livid scar on the left side of my face about the size of a half dollar. Isn't there some way I can overcome this so it won't be so noticeable? My make-up does help, but the scar is still evident.

Helen S.,
Topeka, Kansas.

Answer:—If you will write to my Studio personally, I will be pleased to send you a sample of a special preparation that is applied before make-up which will conceal your scar completely. Please state your complexion and whether your skin is dry or oily.

*American Cinematographer Magazine, October 1929

YOUR MAKE-UP PROBLEMS

DEAR MR. FACTOR:—I am a brunette with light brown eyes, dark hair and olive skin. Two weeks ago, I blondined my hair, the result is that my make-up makes me look grotesque. What can I do?

L.P.,
San Diego, Calif.

ANSWER:—To avoid a clash in the color harmony of your make-up, I would suggest that you carry a much lighter complexion with your make-up. Nature has its own scheme of giving the complexion a harmonizing combination of colors, and this is the standard by which our judgment is governed. Now that you are a blond, I would advise you to use a natural shade of powder in preference to any lighter or darker shades. Blend a brown eye shadow over the lids and use a medium lip rouge, Blondeen dry rouge for the cheeks. This will give you the proper color harmony for the change.

MY DEAR MR. FACTOR:—I recently read in the *Los Angeles Examiner* an article which said that 47 per cent of the women in the United Sates were neither blondes, brunettes nor redheads—that they were Brownettes. That interested me greatly as I am a brownette. I have gray eyes, brown hair and my skin is medium in color. Will you give me your idea of just what I should use to get an effective make-up.

M.C.,
Dayton, Ohio

ANSWER:—Use olive face powder, medium lipstick, gray eye shadow and raspberry dry rouge.

MY DEAR MR. FACTOR:—I am of Spanish extraction and while my hair is blue black and my eyes are very dark, my skin is light and creamy and not olive. You have heard of the Spanish girl of dark skin and blonde hair; I am just the reverse. Will you please tell me how I can overcome this peculiar color scheme and reconcile my complexion to my hair and eyes?

L.M.,
Detroit, Mich.

ANSWER:—I think that a very fair skin against a brunette background is very attractive and if you use a natural powder it would not change your complexion any and harmonize with your own complexion. I would complete your make-up by using a brown eye shadow over the lids, a dark lip rouge and a raspberry dry rouge for the cheeks.

I am a redhead and freckle easy. What can I do to do away with these freckles? Is there a foundation cream that will overcome the freckles so that my make-up can be put on over all and eliminate them?

Laura G.,
New Rochelle

ANSWER:—During my experience I have not found any cream that would remove freckles entirely; however, I suggest that you use a powder foundation that will blend between the shade of your freckles and your natural skin. The powder foundation when properly applied will conceal the freckles effectively.

DEAR MR. FACTOR:—Do you design wigs to suit the wearer's personality? I am very blonde, which of course makes it difficult for me to wear all colors on the stage, successfully, and so I have considered having a dark wig if I could get one which looked like it belonged to me. Also, could you do this from a photograph?

ANSWER:—We want to advise you that we create and design wigs for every personality known to the stage and screen. This cannot be done successfully from a photograph. Hair, in order to appear like it is part of you, must be in harmony with the lines of your contour—your head must be measured very carefully so that the wig will be shaped correctly. Also the color must be in harmony with your complexion.

*American Cinematographer Magazine, *November 1929*

THE KEY TO A BEAUTIFUL COMPLEXION

With the same painstaking research and meticulousness as Factor had used with his color cosmetics, he would apply a similar principle to caring for the skin. After all, much of what he aimed to do was to teach women everywhere to enhance their natural beauty and to make the most of their features by highlighting the good and minimizing flaws and unsightliness. Factor knew that at the root of a beautifully created face was a good skin care regimen. When Society MakeUp was launched, it featured with it a number of cleansers and beauty aids (Skin Tissue

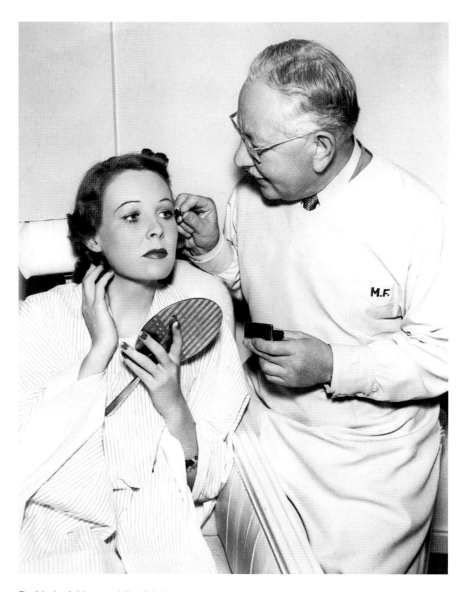

Red-haired, blue-eyed English beauty Wendy Barrie became known during the 1930s for her appearances on the *Jack Haley Radio Show* and for her roles in numerous British films. In this publicity photo, Barrie is the quintessential makeup pupil, wearing a crisp, pinstriped smock and holding a hand mirror as Max Factor delicately applies mascara to her lashes.

NEW ART OF SOCIETY MAKE-UP SKIN CARE REGIMEN

To correct a dry skin. AT NIGHT, cleanse the skin and remove make-up with Max Factor's Melting Cleansing Cream. Apply Max Factor's Skin and Tissue Cream generously and leave on all night so that the nourishing oils will be absorbed by the dry skin.

AT MORNING, refresh the skin with a facial bath of Max Factor's Skin Freshener. Protect the skin for all day with Max Factor's Make-up Foundation.

To correct an oily skin. AT NIGHT, cleanse the face with Melting Cleansing Cream. Apply Max Factor's Astringent to correct the oily condition and to contract the enlarged pores, which usually accompany an oily skin.

AT MORNING, apply Astringent again to counteract oiliness and to close the pores before make-up. Follow with Honeysuckle Cream, which supplements Astringent in correcting the oily condition, and also provides a basis for perfect make-up.

To care for a normal skin. AT NIGHT, cleanse with Max Factor's Melting Cleansing Cream. Nourish with a light application of Max Factor's Skin and Tissue Cream.

AT MORNING, refresh the skin with Max Factor's Skin Freshener, and start your make-up with Max Factor's make-up Foundation.

*From a 1937 Society MakeUp skin care brochure

Cream, Melting Cream Cleanser and others) that addressed everything from scars and freckling to wrinkles and clogged pores. By the end of the 1940s, the company had introduced numerous new treatment products, including Night Facial Stik and Satin Flow Cleansing Cream.

By the 1950s, Max Factor and Company had become prolific in the manufacturing and distribution of its skincare products by launching its Secret Key treatment line. Based on the premise that achieving the correct acid-alkaline balance is the key to radiant skin, Secret Key worked wonders

Though there had been other cosmetics on the market in the early days of filmmaking, Max Factor was the first to invent homeopathic makeup. Up until 1920, many makeup products were toxic, containing mercury, lead and other detrimental contaminates. When actors perspired, the toxins would seep into the pores, causing infection and even death. Factor's Supreme line of products, which included sanitary greasepaint, lip rouge and lip gloss, was completely safe to wear. Max Factor's commitment to chemical-free products would earn him much recognition throughout his career.

on the complexion by removing the contaminants that work as a barrier to moisturizers and night creams penetrating the skin. In addition to the miraculous Secret Key Toner, the line featured complexion-perfecting products, including Double-Depth Cleanser, Active Moisturizer and Velvety Night Cream. The active ingredient within Secret Key and other Max Factor treatment items during this era was lanolin. Max Factor also preached the invaluable ideas of healthy eating, proper sleep and sun protection long before such things had come into the consciousness of the public. All of these early principles are common ideas today, but some ninety years ago, the cosmetics pioneer was far ahead of his time, not minimizing his work to a cake of mascara or a pot of lip rouge, but instead promoting an entire routine with integral parts, each one as important as the other.

A candid image of Carole Lombard. The actress would endorse Max Factor products, appearing in countless advertisements for Color Harmony and Society MakeUp throughout the 1930s and 1940s.

A strawberry blond Carole Lombard poses for a publicity photo, circa 1940.

Above: A display of Max Factor products, including a bottle of Technicolor blood.

Left: Claudette Colbert in an advertisement for Pan-Cake Makeup. The ad serves as publicity, as it coincides with Colbert's newly released film *The Guest Wife*.

WHEN you make up, think of tomorrow as well as today…choose "Pan-Cake", the original, which because of its exclusive patented formula does two things… it creates glamour for today and safeguards the skin against sun and wind which may bring drying, harshening, aging signs tomorrow. Once you try "Pan-Cake", you'll be devoted to it forever *because*…

★ *It creates a lovely new complexion; there's a color harmony shade for your type*

★ *It gives the skin a safer, smoother, younger look; the formula guards against drying*

★ *It takes just a few seconds to make up; and stays on for hours without re-touching*

★ *It helps hide tiny complexion faults; your make-up always looks fresh and lovely*

And remember, there's only one "Pan-Cake", the original, created by *Max Factor Hollywood*. Tested and proved perfect by famous screen stars and millions of lovely girls and women everywhere. Make up with Pan-Cake today for your most thrilling adventure in new beauty.

Claudette Colbert in "GUEST WIFE"
A Jack Skirball Production
United Artists Release

PAN-CAKE*MAKE-UP

AN EXCLUSIVE FORMULA PROTECTED BY U. S. PATENT NOS. 2034697-2101834   *Pan-Cake…Trade Mark Reg. U.S. Pat. Off.

ORIGINATED BY MAX FACTOR HOLLYWOOD

In just 50 seconds Your Complexion can be looking... Smooth, Glamourous, Lovely

with miraculous

PAN-CAKE* MAKE-UP

BY *Max Factor*

HOLLYWOOD

ESTHER WILLIAMS *co-starring* in M-G-M's production "TEXAS CARNIVAL" Color by Technicolor

A dreamy aqua blue advertisement featuring "Million-Dollar Mermaid" Esther Williams. Williams was one of the many actresses to become synonymous with the brand when Factor created a waterproof makeup for the elaborate swim sequences for which her films became famous.

Glamour for you, too...

and a lovelier, younger-looking beauty when you make up with "Pan-Cake", today's make-up fashion

Lana Turner in METRO-GOLDWYN-MAYER'S "WEEK-END at the WALDORF"

★ It creates a lovely new complexion

★ It helps conceal tiny complexion faults

★ It stays on for hours without re-powdering

For a thrilling new adventure in beauty, try this modern make-up..."Pan-Cake". See how easily and quickly it creates a glamorous new complexion, lovely in color, smooth-as-pearl, and flawless...see how it gives your skin a softer, smoother, younger look...note how your make-up remains fresh and lovely for hours without re-powdering. Try "Pan-Cake" just once...and like millions of girls and women you'll be devoted to it forever.

Pan-Cake* Make-Up

AN EXCLUSIVE FORMULA PROTECTED BY U. S. PATENT NOS. 2034697-2161834

"Pan-Cake...Trade Mark Reg. U.S. Pat. Off.

Lana Turner in a 1945 advertisement for Max Factor, which also touts her latest film, *Week-End at the Waldorf*.

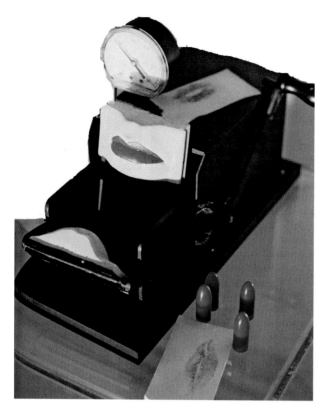

The famed smooch-test apparatus engineered in 1939 by Max Factor Jr. to ensure the indelibility of Tru-Color Lipstick: the Kissing Machine. This ever-important contribution to cosmetics history remains on permanent display at the Hollywood Museum.

During the 1930s, Rita Cansino began endorsing Max Factor's Color Harmony principle of makeup. Later, she would be transformed into a redhead—and Rita Hayworth—achieving superstardom.

Elizabeth Taylor in a 1951 advertisement for Max Factor's Clear Red Lipstick. The ad originally appeared in *Modern Screen*, one of the most popular celebrity fan magazines of the era.

A 1940s portrait of Claudette Colbert.

A Wac gets an intimate glimpse of this Metro-Goldwyn-Mayer motion picture production and visits with Van Johnson and Phyllis Thaxter, who play Capt. and Mrs. Ted W. Lawson, Mervyn LeRoy, the director, and Hal Rosson, the director of photography.

"Women's Army Corps urgently needs you. Join the WAC now"

PAN-CAKE MAKE-UP originated by MAX FACTOR HOLLYWOOD

Remember, there is only one "Pan-Cake", the original, created by *Max Factor Hollywood* for Technicolor Pictures and the Hollywood screen stars, and now the make-up fashion with millions of girls and women.

An advertisement for the 1944 film *Thirty Seconds Over Tokyo*. The World War II drama, which starred Spencer Tracey, epitomizes the era of Technicolor film.

Max Factor Pan-Cake Makeup. Launched in 1939, Pan-Cake set the industry standard for all cinematic makeup from that point forward.

A youthful Angela Lansbury
promoting Max Factor
Makeup in 1946.

Jaclyn Smith was
not only one of
the most iconic
faces to represent
Max Factor during
the 1970s and
1980s, but she
also appeared
in hundreds of
commercials
and print ads
for the brand,
such as this one
for Max Factor's
Skin Principle
Moisturizer in 1982.

Left: A selection of handsome autographed gift sets by Max Factor in a 1944 issue of *Hollywood* magazine. Choices included Vanity Cologne and Talc set, Color Harmony Makeup set, Vanity Lipstick set and others, with prices ranging from $1.00 to $9.55.

Below: Janet Blair promotes Pan-Cake Makeup and her latest film, *Gallant Journey*, for *Modern Screen* magazine in 1946.

Marguerite Chapman, star of Columbia Pictures' *The Walls Came Tumbling Down*, giving Pan-Cake a plug in a 1948 issue of *Modern Screen* magazine.

Actress Ann Sothern demonstrating Max Factor's "Cream-Type Make-Up in the smart swivel stik" for *Modern Screen* magazine in 1948. Sothern co-starred in MGM's *Words and Music*, which coincided with the ad.

Above: Actress Jane Greer for "Hollywood's Ultra Smooth Make-Up" in 1951.

Left: Shelley Winters in *Modern Screen* magazine promoting "the lipstick secret of Hollywood stars who must have a lipstick that really stays on…that's non-drying…that always looks beautiful and appealing."

While the use of Hollywood stars in Max Factor ads was prolific during the 1930s and throughout the 1940s and '50s, this issue of *Modern Screen* magazine from 1952 offers a unique look at an unknown model in an ad for Pan-Cake Makeup.

Merle Oberon, star of *Wuthering Heights*, appears in a 1939 issue of *Photoplay* magazine in an ad for Max Factor Lipstick.

Above, left: The sultry Betty Hutton, star of Paramount Pictures' *Let's Face It*, appears in this 1943 advertisement for Max Factor's Tru-Color Lipstick.

Above, right: Actress Maureen O'Hara in a 1943 issue of *Screenland* magazine. O'Hara, star of a RKO-Radio's *This Land Is Mine*, lends her face to Max Factor for Tru-Color Lipstick.

Left: Actress Evelyn Keyes for Color Harmony Makeup; this advertisement appeared in a 1948 issue of *Screenland* magazine and was publicity for Keyes's latest film, *The Mating of Millie*.

Joan Leslie promoting Max Factor Clear Red Lipstick. The ad originally appeared in a 1948 issue of *Screenland* magazine and offered three alluring shades of crimson: Clear Red, Blue Red and Rose Red.

Rita Hayworth, star of Columbia Pictures' *The Loves of Carmen*, appears in a 1948 issue of *Screenland* magazine for "Hollywood's Newest Glamour Secret," Pan-Stik Makeup.

Barbara Stanwyck

Anne Shirley in RKO-Radio's "HAPPY HOLIDAY"

Max Factor ★ Hollywood Face Powder!

1..it imparts a lovely color to the skin
2..it creates a satin-smooth make-up
3..it clings perfectly...really stays on

HERE IS the famous face powder created in Color Harmony Shades for each type...*blonde, brunette, brownette and redhead*...that will give your complexion a lovely, youthful-looking color tone. Try your Color Harmony Shade of Max Factor Hollywood Face Powder today...one dollar.

MAX FACTOR HOLLYWOOD COLOR HARMONY MAKE-UP
...FACE POWDER, ROUGE AND TRU-COLOR LIPSTICK

Above: A leopard-adorned Barbara Stanwyck in the March 1944 issue of *Screenland* magazine. Stanwyck advertises Max Factor's Tru-Color lipstick, as well as her upcoming film, *Double Indemnity*.

Left: Anne Shirley in a September 1935 issue of *Screenland* magazine for Max Factor Face Powder.

An advertisement for gifts for blondes, brunettes, brownettes and redheads.

Maureen O' Hara promotes Max Factor Hollywood lipstick and her latest film, *Sinbad, the Sailor*.

MAX FACTOR sets your lips aglow with
IRIDESCENT MAGIC
new luminous lipstick brings them excitingly
alive with soft shimmering beauty

An unknown print model promotes Max Factor Iridescent Magic Lipstick, circa 1950s.

Debbie Reynolds, circa 1960. The beautiful, fresh-faced star of *Singin' in the Rain* and *The Unsinkable Molly Brown* would be among the last celebrities to grace Max Factor's print advertisements when the studio system started its decline in the 1950s.

FACTOR CALIBRATES BEAUTY

Constantly seeking to enhance the natural beauty of the feminine face, Factor would branch out beyond color cosmetics and skin care in 1932, and this time it would be something that could have been mistaken for a medieval torturing device. Max Factor believed there were two very specific things to look for when analyzing any woman's beauty: the height of the forehead and the nose should be of a particular measurement, and the separation space between the eyes should be the exact width of one eye. What's more, when the faces of the actresses appear on the enormous movie screen, Factor was of the opinion that any defects that can be seen with the naked eye run the risk of being a huge distraction to moviegoers. Knowing that this kind of potential calamity wouldn't do, Max invented a way to play up the strong features and minimize the flaws when making up his leading ladies. It was with this scientific research that Factor invented the Beauty Micrometer.

Also known as the Beauty Calibrator, the apparatus was designed specifically to analyze the face and highlight which regions needed to be corrected, enhanced, minimized and showcased. When placed over the entire head and face, leaving only the neck exposed, the device, which contained more than three hundred adjustable screws—and just as many adjustments—allowed for a comprehensive examination of a woman's facial features and, thus, analyzed her true beauty. Although Factor's device had originally been intended for use in the film industry, the cosmetics guru had high hopes that his calibrator would eventually be a permanent fixture in salons across the country. While the unique contraption had served its purpose of analyzing the facial dimensions of movie stars (its unusual aesthetic had made headlines all over the world), it would never reach the widespread popularity and use Max had first envisioned. Today, it remains on permanent collection at the Hollywood Museum and is one of the most well-known and memorable beauty mechanisms ever to be invented.

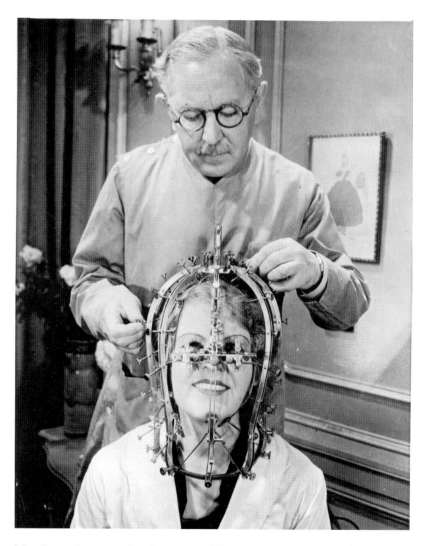

Max Factor demonstrating the renowned Beauty Calibrator on actress Marjorie
Reynolds in 1934.

Chapter 7
PAN-CAKE

M ax Factor had solved a huge dilemma years earlier during the transition from orthochromatic to panchromatic film with his revolutionary Panchromatic Makeup. Softening the appearance of actors and thus complementing their features had been a relief to studio executives, not to mention stars and their egos. But when the industry made the leap from panchromatic to Technicolor, Hollywood was reluctant to jump on the bandwagon. While studio heads were apprehensive because of the high financial cost of filming in Technicolor (going bankrupt was an unfortunate reality during this time), actors boycotted it for another reason altogether. Fearing a ghastly appearance when seen through the lens of the Technicolor camera, many leading ladies would staunchly say no to the new medium, if only in the beginning.

Engineered for the first time in 1916, two-strip Technicolor had been the most color-saturated process in filmmaking so far. The 1920s would see the development of three-strip Technicolor, which used a full range of bright, vibrant color. Still, due to the expense of shooting in the lavish new medium, the process was often reserved for key film sequences only, such as action or fight scenes. With the onset of the Great Depression and Hollywood producers looking to cut corners any way they could, it would be some time before three-strip Technicolor would flourish.

Walt Disney would be among the first to fully employ the use of Technicolor, using it to produce a number of cartoon shorts beginning with its *Silly Symphonies* series in 1932. Shortly after, the company would sign an exclusive agreement, producing all of its cartoons—which were quickly growing in popularity—in Technicolor. That same year, the first

A young man working in the laboratory in 1928. His industrial-weight apron reveals the seriousness of the business of beauty product manufacturing.

Max Factor and an employee inspect Tru-Color Lipstick in 1932. The apparatus they're working with—used for either counting or organizing—was one of the many high-tech devices utilized by Max Factor and Company to streamline the operation.

Technicolor Process 4 Camera was invented. No matter the cost, one thing was unanimous: movies simply looked better in Technicolor. But what to put on the faces of matinee idols was still the rub. Luckily, Max Factor had been hard at work patenting something that would change the faces of movie stars and everyday women for decades to come.

VOGUES OF *1938*

With the help of his son Frank, Max Factor would work to create a brand-new formula that would not only be compatible with Technicolor but would also beautify the actresses to whom he catered. They considered a number of issues during the experimentation process, taking into account everything from texture and breathability to coverage and application. Color and shade had been key to the process, as they would be added to Factor's scientific Color Harmony range. After nearly two years of testing and experimenting, the Factors introduced "Pan-Cake" to Hollywood.

It has been sad that the product was dubbed "Pan" because it came in a container shaped like a pan and "Cake" because the consistency was similar to that of a cake. Other accounts have said "Pan" was to represent the word "panchromatic," though the first suggestion seems more plausible since panchromatic had already been outmoded by this time. Whatever the case, Max Factor's glorious Pan-Cake Makeup made its official debut in 1938—to rave reviews. Though it had had been first created in 1935 and used, in part, in a number of Technicolor films, *Vogues of 1938*, starring Joan Bennett (Bennett had replaced a still Technicolor-shy Carole Lombard, who was originally slated for the role), was the first feature film produced in Technicolor to utilize Pan-Cake Makeup throughout the entire movie on all of the actors. The makeup was so revolutionary and had gained so much attention that *Vogues of 1938* was the first film where critics gave as much consideration to the makeup as they did to the acting and directing. Of the landmark new invention, one critic wrote, "Never before in a color motion picture have the players looked so natural and realistic. They were so lifelike, in fact, that it seemed like they would step down from the screen into the audience at any minute."

And like so many of his products had done previously, Pan-Cake would set the standard for makeup within all color motion pictures from that point on, becoming synonymous with the motion picture industry. Even actresses previously dead-set against being filmed in Technicolor embraced it. The makeup was so sought after that models and movie extras began taking it home

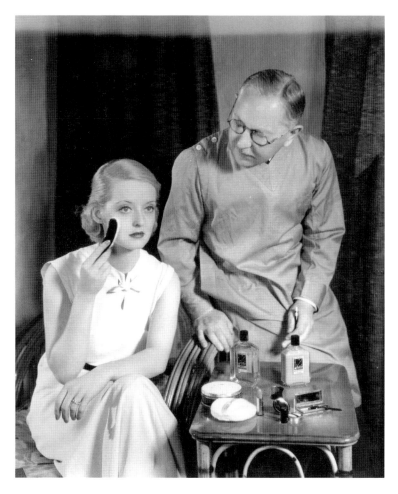

This 1930s photo remains one of the most iconic photographs of Bette Davis and Max Factor. It reveals an often-unseen softer side of the hard-boiled actress, whose youth and radiance in this image almost make her convincing as ingénue.

with them in large quantities—it was reported at the time that up to $2,000 worth was taken off the set every week—to use in their daily lives. However, they soon learned that the makeup could be worn only at night because it appeared too dark. They begged Max Factor to create a formula for daytime, but he always refused. He had created Pan-Cake strictly for use in motion pictures. That, too, would eventually change with his son Frank's creation of something that would have just as big of an impact some years later. Still available today, Pan-Cake Makeup not only remains one of Max Factor's original products created for cinema, but women still love to use it for its transformative benefits to the texture and appearance of their skin.

"A woman who doesn't wear lipstick feels undressed in public. Unless she works on a farm."
—Max Factor

A group of young ingénues being instructed on the proper way to apply lipstick. The blond "model" on the right is Judy Garland one year before she made her feature film debut in 20th Century Fox's *Pigskin Parade*.

Chapter 8

CREATING BEAUTY

Actresses adored Max Factor. It was with them in mind that he had designed the finest beauty products in the world; they were the barometers by which he measured each new item. Factor stuck to one rule: if his actresses liked it, he would launch it to the public, as other women were sure to want it, too. It was with this tried-and-true method that he brought forth so many new inventions, beginning with Lip Pomade—it would later be reengineered as Lip Gloss—in 1928. Previously, actresses would be asked by the director to lick their lips in order to achieve a moistened, dewy effect on camera. Factor's Lip Pomade would solve the problem, allowing for ongoing moisturized, supple lips. Taking his years of wig-making expertise to another level, Factor engineered false eyelashes—he custom made the first known set of lush human hair cils for actress Phyllis Haver—a look Katharine Hepburn, Marlene Dietrich, Lucille Ball and many other glamorous women would later make their trademarks. He created another innovative idea in his skin brightener (a precursor to the countless primers and illuminators of today) with Supreme Liquid Whitener, which allowed the actor's complexion to appear brighter, smoother and even more flawless on film. And it wasn't just his cosmetic inventions for which he was known; Factor would work hand in hand with movie studios to craft the images of the most unforgettable faces to ever grace the silver screen.

Gamine beauty Colleen Moore's short, fashion-forward "Dutch Bob" was created by Max in order to divert the attention away from her eyes, which were two different colors. With one blue eye and the other brown, Factor designed a hairstyle that would deflect the color variation and, in turn, launch her into superstardom. The fashionable hairstyle defined the Jazz Age and was emulated by women all over the world.

An ash blond Harlean Carpenter was working steadily in motion pictures. Her manager mom—known as "Mama Jean"—had her daughter's name officially changed, and though "Jean Harlow" signed to Howard Hughes's production company, she had yet to make her breakthrough. Max Factor would change her dishwater blond tresses to a never-before-seen shade of blond that he named "platinum." With Harlow's attention-grabbing transformation coinciding with the release of her 1931 film *Hell's Angels*, she became an instant icon.

Fearing she'd become "just another Hollywood blonde," Max Factor would be the one to turn a dark blond–haired Lucille Ball into a redhead. The crimson mane not only went hand in hand with the actress's razor-sharp wit and hilarious comedic shtick for which she was becoming known, but Factor's creation would also catapult her to superstardom. Former Ziegfeld girl Mary Dooley became known for playing femme fatale roles. Although Dooley would change her name to the more dramatic Nita Naldi, the Irish girl from a working-class family still needed a trademark look. Factor invented the "Vampire Lip" for Naldi. As a result, the actress, whose look was often described as "darkly beautiful," would become one of the biggest stars of the silent film era.

Giving her the irresistible "Rosebud Lip" and transforming her thick mane of curls into a shorter, more chic 'do, Factor turned actress Clara Bow into the "it girl." In her films, Bow would embody the freewheeling spirit of the 1920s flapper with her dark, wild curls, gorgeous face and devil-may-care attitude.

When a young Greta Lovisa Gustafsson first arrived in Hollywood, her studio promptly sent her to see Max Factor. He would experiment for ten days, analyzing and assessing the features of the Swedish beauty. In his research, he deduced that her large, dreamy eyes were her best feature. Factor decided that, so as not to detract from her beauty, her lashes would be enhanced with only mascara, not false eyelashes. Not only would he usher in "the natural look" with the actress who would emerge as Greta Garbo, but also the chic, understated makeup style would serve as her trademark for the rest of her career.

A $1,000 public renaming contest held by MGM head Louis B. Mayer turned unknown contract player Lucille LeSueur into Joan Crawford. But the former chorus girl still needed a signature look.

Not wanting to give her the same "Cupid's Bow" lip he'd already created for America's sweetheart Clara Bow, Factor went back to his drawing board. For the actress, he would invent the bold "Hunter's Bow" lip. Characterized by its broad outline of the upper lip, which the makeup guru spread over the Cupid's Bow, the look also became known as "the Smear." The daring style would generate an entire new genre for Crawford, not to mention scads of movie roles and legions of fans.

While brunette beauty Hedy Lamarr was said by Factor to have needed "the least corrective make-up applied compared to all of the other actresses," Dolores Del Rio, he declared, "has less use for eye make-up than any other beauty." And it wasn't just actresses whose careers he transformed. A grateful Bing Crosby (who had been both a friend and client of Factor) wrote a personal note to the cosmetics king in 1934, singing the praises of "grease," saying, "Dear Sir, Just to let you know how much I appreciate the new grease. It goes on much faster, feels a lot better, is easier on my skin and photographs 100% better."

Like his father, Max Factor Jr. appreciated the beauty of each varying hair and eye color, the diversity and sublimity of all skin complexions, of every high cheekbone and strong brow bone, and be it of Scandinavian or Egyptian descent, Creole or Filipino, Max possessed the ability to maximize the exquisiteness and natural beauty of every single face. According to Factor, "The perfect American woman" would be composed of all nationalities and races. As he once told a reporter, "She would have deep blue Scandinavian eyes…give her the luxuriant brows and lashes of the Latins, the prominent cheek structure of Indians from our New England states, a rugged Celtic mouth and lips and the imperious jaw line and carriage of the patrician English type.

IMAGE AND IMITATION

Since its earliest beginnings, Max Factor and Company upheld the idea that playing up a woman's most attractive features was the basis of true glamour and that any woman could be attractive if she followed a few simple rules. In addition to always striving for as natural of a look as possible, Max Factor had a number of basic, but ever-important rules to always consider in order to achieve one's most glamorous self. In an October 1950 interview with *Swing* magazine, Factor Jr. explains how to attain the same exquisite look as the movie stars. The tips he gives are advice that was timely for the era and, at the same time, ageless, applying as much today as they did more than six decades ago:

> *Underapply rather than overapply cosmetics. Never copy a person's appearance in its entirety. If you are short and dumpy for instance, do not imitate Esther Williams. If you insist on copying someone, be sure you are at least a counterpart of the person in age and physical appearance. Cheek rouge ought to be used for corrective purposes, not just coloring. If your face is too full and round, or your cheekbones too prominent, you can pattern the rouge to shadow down defects to a minimum. Even a slight double chin can be minimized by applying rouge on the saggy area. Put lipstick more durably by following the motion picture technique. Apply as usual. Blot off excess with make-up tissue. The powder will serve to cover much of the oil base in the lipstick. Now, very lightly and thinly go over that application with lipstick, which should be applied with a brush. Blot again with make-up tissue. Never forget that your teeth are just as important as your other features. No matter how pretty you are, you are not your best if tobacco stains or lipstick smudges mar your teeth. Whatever your special make-up problems may be, use cosmetics only to enhance your natural beauty, never to obliterate it.*

Unlike eyeglass wearing today, the 1950s offered few—if any—styles aside from that of the horn-rimmed "coke-bottle" variety. Perceived as geeky and awkward, donning spectacles midcentury was more of a social stigma than it was a fashion statement. Even Marilyn Monroe's seemingly flighty but shrewd bombshell Lorelei Lee summed up the sentiment of spectacles in *Gentlemen Prefer Blondes*, declaring, "Men seldom make passes at girls who wear glasses." Still, Max Factor offered a solution in this arena, saying:

> *You can be glamorous with glasses. If wearing glasses of any magnifying power, do your eye-make-up extra carefully. If magnifying power is great, you would do better to eliminate eye make-up altogether.*

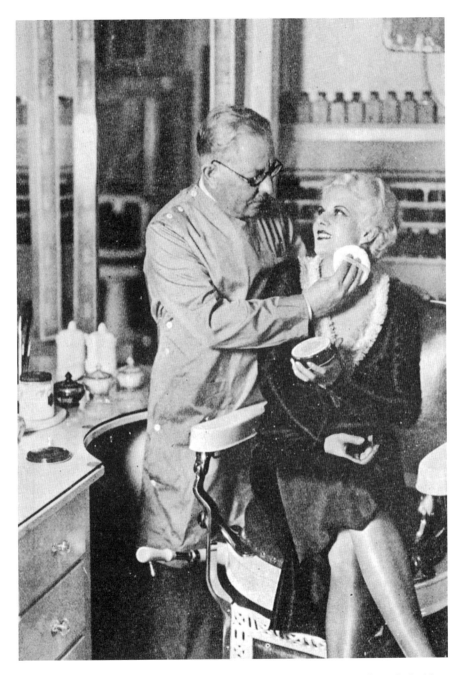

Jean Harlow and Max Factor in a 1930s publicity photo. The famous blonde worked with Factor extensively throughout her career; it was said that she admired his work as much as she did him as a person.

Actress Anna May Wong at the Max Factor Salon in Hollywood, 1924. Wong spent her childhood dreaming of a career in the movies. Born and raised in Los Angeles, the exotic beauty would overcome the deep-seated racism that plagued Hollywood, becoming the first "Americanized Chinese" movie star (Wong preferred to be called, not "American" or "Chinese American," but instead "Americanized Chinese") to achieve international stardom.

Chinese American actress Florence Ung leans in as Max Factor applies lipstick to actress Movita Castaneda in 1937. Despite the lack of ethnically diverse roles for women, Castaneda—who later became Mrs. Marlon Brando—appeared in films such as *Mutiny on the Bounty* in 1935, while Ung appeared in the immensely popular "Charlie Chan" detective films, including *Charlie Chan at the Circus* in 1936 and *Charlie Chan in Honolulu* in 1938.

Dramatic silent film actress Nita Naldi wearing the unforgettable "Vampire Lip" created expressly for her by Max Factor.

An au naturale Jean Harlow before her transformation to platinum blonde.

"Stars would come into the Max Factor building for makeup consultations and wig fittings if they were working on a film. There, they would have their own private makeup rooms. It was a very elaborate process, and the studio paid for it. A large truck would drive into the alley behind the building and onto the giant elevator, where it was loaded up with all of the wonderful cosmetics, and drive it back to the movie studio for the star. It was all very scientific; it was super professional. Max Factor was ahead of his time."
—Marc Wanamaker

Chapter 9

THE GLAMOUR FACTORY

Since arriving in Los Angeles in the fall of 1908, Max Factor's one-man wig and greasepaint business had grown exponentially. Naturally, rapid growth of the burgeoning beauty business called for expansion. What had started in a small store on Central Avenue would be vacated for larger spaces, not once, but three times total—first to the prestigious Pantages Building in downtown LA's theater district and, later, to 326 South Hill Street, also located downtown. In 1928, after purchasing a large four-story building that had previously housed the Hollywood Storage Company, Max Factor would move up to 1666 North Highland Avenue in the heart of Tinsel Town. The new space would be christened on March 22, 1928, with a small ceremony. Just as his previous locations had, the elegant new salon would cater to models and movie stars—at least for a time. The stock market crash in October 1929—and the onset of the Great Depression—would halt Max's plans for a major renovation until several years later. Though hard times had befallen the entire country, Max and his beauty empire were able to ride out much of the severely depressed financial downturn unscathed.

When the time was right, the makeup guru hired famed architect S. Charles Lee (Lee had designed some of LA's grandest movie palaces, including the "finest thousand-seat theater in America," the Tower Theater) to turn his Highland Avenue studio into a full-fledged glamour factory. Lee would take the building's lackluster façade and fashion it into a neoclassical art deco masterpiece. The exterior boasted lavish green marble, sconces of brass and glass, and signs above each ornately carved window alcove reading "Hairgoods, Wigs, Toupees." The sterling silver signage above the entrance read "Max Factor Makeup Studio." Ornately dressed windows that featured tantalizing displays with the latest products lined Highland Avenue, which would become a must-see for shoppers and eager lookie-loos hoping to catch a glimpse of a real movie star. Lee would also add on to the existing structure an additional salon containing eighteen full-service beauty stations; the extra space would become frequented by lesser-known actresses, as well as everyday women in need of hair appointments or makeovers. Inside, the four-story beauty palace boasted a sweeping marble stair entry and marble flooring, gold-leaf accents, a color palette featuring six different shades of pink and mauve and built-in display cases chock-full of Max Factor's latest beauty wares.

INVITATION ONLY

November 26, 1935, marked the grand opening of Max Factor's glamour factory. The party was intended for three thousand guests, though more than eight thousand people lined the streets hoping to gain entrance to the soirée. A beauty bash Hollywood style, the invitation-only affair went down in history as being the largest nontheatrical event that had ever taken place.

Claudette Colbert, Ginger Rogers and Judy Garland were only some of the countless celebrities on hand to celebrate and sign what remains the biggest collection of autographs to date: the Scroll of Fame. The scroll would also be autographed by notorious rival gossip columnists Hedda Hopper and Louella Parsons, who signed at opposite ends.

Stars arrived via limousine, each one stopping to be photographed with Max Factor and to speak to the press. Every part of the sparkling new beauty palace was equipped to the hilt, with live beauticians doing beauty demonstrations on models. Every floor served a purpose—from pulverizing machines, wig-making and barbering services to manicuring, packaging and shipping, the factory was in full effect. The top floor was used to mix color for powders, rouge and eye shadow; explosive charges used during the process left a metallic residue, something Factor would later use to invent shimmer eye shadow. The second floor was where hair

Your presence is cordially requested to a private party for notables of the film industry to include a preview of Max Factor's new make-up studio, Tuesday afternoon and evening, 1666 N. Highland Avenue, Hollywood, Cal. Cocktails and entertainment from four to ten.

Invitation to the 1935 opening of the Max Factor Makeup Studio

color products were manufactured, the third floor was for lipstick making (it was the official birthplace of tube lipstick) and the main floor was the showroom and retail store.

Factor, always striving for the perfect hair and makeup combination, would create four specially colored rooms, epitomizing his Color Harmony principle. The state-of-the-art air-conditioned rooms contained sinks, mirrored lights, dressing tables, hot and cold running water, settees and any and all accoutrements to make comfortable the bombshells to whom he catered. At the opening night festivities, Jean Harlow would christen the powder blue "For Blondes Only" room, Rochelle Hudson cut the ribbon for the peach-colored "For Brownettes Only" room, Claudette Colbert would do the honors in the pink "For Brunettes Only" room and Ginger Rogers, the mint-green "For Redheads Only" room. In the weeks and months to come, Max Factor would crank out beauty products and signature looks one after another. Of the four-story beauty factory, Donelle Dadigan, owner and president of the Hollywood Museum, says:

> *In fact, women during that time period weren't born better looking than the women are today. Women would walk into the building looking like everyday people and walk out looking like screen goddesses. Max Factor was very good at what he did. He was a makeup and lighting genius. Max made it acceptable to wear make-up. He changed the way women—and society looked at being made up. Before Max Factor, women would pinch their cheeks and purse their lips to get a little bit of color. For the first time, shopkeepers, secretaries and teachers could*

come into the front lobby and buy make-up without being judged or looked down upon. Another very big part of the allure of course, was also that they could see movie stars when they came in. The opening of Max Factor in Hollywood had a huge cultural impact. It changed the way the world viewed makeup.

A LASTING MYSTIQUE

Years after the studio system had waned and the golden era had passed, noted historian Marc Wanamaker would experience the place that had represented the Hollywood glamour machine for decades:

By the 1970s, the studio system had been over for a long time; the decline had really started during 1950s. I worked for the American Film Institute as a production liaison from 1970 until 1977. There was a very small group of directors, editors and cameramen, and I worked with all of them. They would make mostly small films, very high quality, very artistic and very experimental in nature. As production liaison, one of my many jobs was to take the newly exposed film directly to the lab in Hollywood—to CFI Labs, which stood for Consolidated Film Industries, a place that dated back to the silent film industry. I would take the film and go meet with the lab managers. I was always given explicit instructions.

I helped set up the editing rooms. One of the jobs I worked on was a film by Stanton Kaye, and it was a western. It was a 35mm feature, shooting on location in Technicolor. In those days, Technicolor had a deal with AFI. The blood they used must be a special Technicolor blood. Of course, Max Factor had designed a special blend of cinematic blood specifically for Technicolor during the 1930s; it appeared very, very real on film. I was sent to the Max Factor building to get the blood. I'd driven by the building hundreds of times—and the place was literally a factory. I walked up to the front entrance, which was very grand. The outside had this beautiful marble and beautiful displays in each window. I made my way into the lobby and told them I was there to pick up some Technicolor blood for a particular film. There was a special room where they made the blood, which, by the way, was considered a cosmetic, and it was also homeopathic—as were many of Max Factor's cosmetics. His products wouldn't burn the skin and

Right: The Max Factor building at 1666 North Highland Avenue in 1932.

Below: The building after architect S. Charles Lee's lavish renovation.

contained no toxins. Max Factor had used special chemicals in this kind of blood, so it would come out red on film. And it did come out red—a red that looked exactly like real blood.

Companies had had a very hard time for years when it came to cinematic blood; they had a very hard time trying to find something that looked authentic. Other studios had their own version of blood. There was one kind of blood for non-Technicolor and also one that was used for black-and-white film. Once I entered the building, they led me to the back. There was a giant elevator, which was used to connect the floors for wigs, cosmetics and other departments. They brought me into the room where the blood was kept. They gave me really detailed instructions, like not to let the blood be exposed to the sun, the temperature it needed to be stored at and things like that. I brought the blood back to the studio and watched them apply it. I learned so much about filmmaking, how Max Factor fit into the scheme of things and what an impact he had made in makeup and in motion pictures.

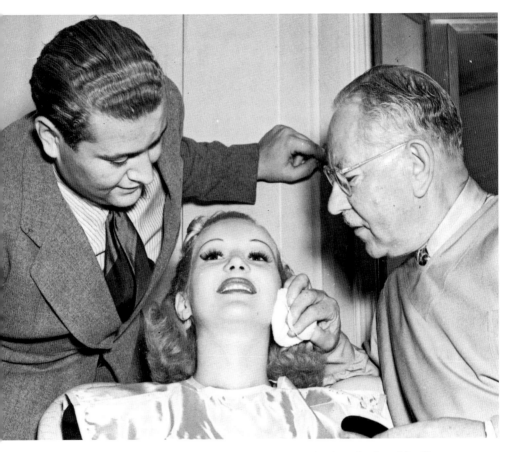

Women all over the country weren't the only ones interested in knowing how Max Factor worked his magic. In 1937, Italian director and producer Vittorio Mussolini—son of Il Duce, Benito Mussolini—would visit Tinsel Town to learn the art of makeup application as instructed by Max Factor. In this publicity photo, Betty Grable poses as Max's model while Mussolini observes.

Actor Edward G. Robinson made a name for himself playing roles that ranged from tough guy to comedian. In true life, the actor was soft spoken and studious. Here, Robinson is pictured with Mr. Factor and his wife, Gladys, in 1935 at the Max Factor Makeup Studio in Hollywood.

Actress Marsha Hunt during the filming of *Hollywood Boulevard* in 1936. Despite her immense popularity (she appeared in fifty-two films throughout her career), Hunt would be among the dozens of actors and screenwriters to end up on the House Un-American Activities Committee (HUAC). Hunt and her fellow actors (Lauren Bacall and Humphrey Bogart among them) would take part in a star-studded radio program *Hollywood Fights Back* to defend the rights to creativity that had been taken from the community. Though she was named as a potential communist along with more than 150 others, Hunt, who was told to back down if she wanted more work, refused. Her blacklist status would make it difficult for her to find acting roles in the years that followed the hearings.

Max Factor poses at his studio in Hollywood with a group of young models. *From left to right*: Dorothy Brown, Dorothy Dalton, Margaret Hehn, Caroline Oliver, Frances Noble and Helen Dax.

"I remember going to the Max Factor building and being made up there for a shoot I was doing. Walking through the building, there was a sense that you were walking back into the past to a time that held a kind of magic. That golden era time was more glamorous than any other time. The actresses had a sense of mystery around them. And people dreamed about them. They wondered about them. The women were made up perfectly. It was a precise look; a porcelain doll look. And Max Factor created it."

—Jaclyn Smith

The extensive wig operation at the Max Factor building in Hollywood, 1940.

Chapter 10

FOR RENT

M ax Factor had been practicing the art of wig making since his youth back in Russia. By the time he arrived in Los Angeles, at the age of thirty-six, he was a veteran when it came to the craft of wig artistry. In his first shop on Central Avenue, Factor would stock well-known brands of stage makeup, experiment with his own formulations and, like he'd come up through the ranks doing, making wigs, switches, toupees and hairpieces.

In 1913, the filming of the elaborate western *The Squaw Man* began. The film had been slated for production in Arizona, but because of the lack of variety within the Sonoran Desert, producers ventured to Los Angeles, where it would be filmed in its entirety. *The Squaw Man* was directed by Cecil B. DeMille and Oscar Apfel and starred Dustin Farnum, one of the most popular leading men of the silent film era.

The Squaw Man was just one of many films that would be produced that year, and although movies during this period were being churned out by the dozens, not unlike makeup, the makeshift hairpieces worn by the actors left much to be desired. Actors' homespun versions of hair made use of everything from upholstery stuffing and peat moss to mulch and tobacco. Factor knew there was a major need for improvement with the kinds of options to which actors had resorted. He also knew that producers had few extra dollars available in their budgets to purchase his finely crafted hairpieces, but he would approach DeMille anyhow. And while the director confirmed Max's fears about the lack of finances, not all was lost.

THOUGH DUSTIN FARNUM WOULD HAVE a successful movie career, he passed up an offer from DeMille to pay him with a combination of cash and the chance to invest $5,000 in the film. Laughing off the paltry offer, Farnum threw the perceived crumbs to his valet. As fate would have it, the stock would skyrocket upon the film's release in 1914, and Farnum's valet became an instant millionaire with the very stock his boss had mocked.

DeMille suggested that Factor rent the wigs and hairpieces to the production each day, receiving a daily rate for their use. Though apprehensive at first—he couldn't imagine his intricately woven human hair wigs being abused from the demands of even one day on a movie set—Factor agreed to rent the wigs to DeMille so long as someone could ensure their intact return at the end of each day. Max's three sons—Frank, Davis and Louis—were employed as extras on the film as Indians in order to keep count and inventory of all their dad's wigs, collecting them for safe keeping at the end of each shooting day. Not only would Max get his wigs back in the same condition as he'd left them, but he also helped develop a lifelong relationship with DeMille and eventually other producers. His wigs would become among the most in-demand items of all his goods from that point on. Of the wig-renting stint, a 1950s article on the subject read:

> *Max Jr., Davis and Louis—the Factor sons—received their movie baptism by fire by going in as extras for $3 a day. Actually, their job was to keep track of the precious hairpieces that had been let out, minus the usual deposit. Many a night, the boys stayed after "shooting" to search a deserted studio lot for wigs that "Indian" extras had torn from their heads and tossed in all directions.*

BEWIGGED BEAUTIES

The wig department at Highland Avenue would become something of a spectacle, and by 1950, it was hands down the largest anywhere in the world. Shelves stacked one on top of another with hairpieces of all varieties lined the walls. In his book, Fred Basten tells how the wig molds were made of the super-high-quality balsa tree wood. A round-toed wooden shoe was used to achieve perfect shape for beards, moustaches goatees and other facial hair creations. Stars came one after another to the studio for wig fittings for their latest films. Each style would be sketched, designed and sent to the crafting department, where ventilators meticulously and painstakingly applied strands, one by one, until another authentic hairpiece was complete.

Another innovation allowing for a look of total authenticity was the advent of the hair-lace wig. Photographing exactly like real hair, the lace-front creation was made with each strand of hair woven into the lace so intricately that one could not tell where the natural hairline stopped and started, making it undetectable on camera and creating a completely natural look. One reporter described his observations of the grueling process during a visit to the Max Factor Makeup Studio in 1936:

> *Into a lace is tied each individual hair. The workers in making the lace wigs earn their paychecks by spending the hours fixing and knotting hair after hair into a piece of lace. In doing this their hands do a quick twisting motion and there the hair is all neatly tied into place. I tried to count the hair one of the girls tied in an hour but when I got around 200 I became tired.*

Just as he had with his cosmetics, Factor considered quality to be of utmost importance. All wigs were made from 100 percent authentic human hair, and all of the hair was imported from Europe. Because he went to such lengths to secure the highest-quality hair, Factor could command top dollar from the studios. The craftsmanship that went into each hairpiece drove the value up even more, with each one requiring hundreds of thousands of strands of hair—nearly 150,000 for a single wig. Technicians at Max Factor worked under unusually bright lamps in order to ensure the installation of each strand was nothing less than perfect. This kind of dedication to excellence no doubt came from Max's days of working under the ultra-discriminating eye of the czar of Russia, and there was no shortage in the demand for wigs during this time in Hollywood. It was the era of the period drama, a time when big-budget spectacle films dominated the silver screen. Epic films such as *Romeo and Juliet, Mutiny on the Bounty, Gone with the Wind* and others required major historical accuracy and authenticity when it came to costumes, wigs and makeup. A 1930s article from the *International Photographer* magazine describes the rigors of wig making:

With Hollywood going into a cycle of costume films, the Wig Department of Max Factor has had to go without lunch and take up its belt another notch or two in order to get the thousands of wigs ready on time. The many recent costume films have each required a special wig.

Factor would overcome another issue that desperately needed attention. The gray- and white-tinted wigs that had worked with panchromatic film came across with a blue tint on the Technicolor camera. Just as he'd done with makeup, Max would return to the proverbial drawing board to engineer a solution: the Technicolor wig. Factor and his team of highly skilled professionals figured out that manipulating the color tints within the wigs and hairpieces even the smallest amount allowed them to read true to color on camera. Factor would receive critical acclaim for the advancement of Technicolor within motion pictures—a feat of epic proportions for an industry that was constantly undergoing changes.

In addition to technological innovations, Max and his team of experts created some of the most memorable looks of all time, including Norma Shearer's regal crown of curls for *Marie Antoinette* and Billie Burke's crimson-colored tresses for Glinda the Good Witch in *The Wizard of Oz*. Factor would also create the caramel-colored mane of the skittish and loveable Cowardly Lion in the film. He brought visual appeal (and a whole lot of sparkle) to Marlene Dietrich's on screen looks by designing drop-dead glamorous wigs for the actress, each one sprinkled with fourteen-karat gold dust—and not just any gold. Dietrich would specify *compressed* gold, which cost upward of sixty dollars an ounce.

A LOYAL FOLLOWING

Max Factor's wigs may have been expensive, but the studios found the extra money spent to be well worth it. Once word had gotten out about the unbelievable quality of his work, producers would begin automatically adding Factor's pricey hairpieces into the cost as a regular part of their budgets. It would have cost far more in time and money to spend the hours it would have taken to stop shooting while a stylist attempted to re-create an elaborate coif each time a new scene was being shot.

Producers, executives and movie stars all loved Max's wigs, as they guaranteed the perfect look every time. Leading ladies who wanted

By the 1950s, Max Factor's wig department had become the largest anywhere in world. Here, Max Factor and three technicians demonstrate their wig-making prowess as they craft a giant hairpiece for a publicity stunt.

extra oomph when off camera made a beeline for Max Factor. Leading men also became some of his most loyal customers, often going to Max personally for their toupees (John Wayne wouldn't think of being seen in public without one of Factor's expertly crafted toupees). Although it was well before the days of the paparazzi and the no-privacy policy experienced by the stars of today, still, celebrities strived to be discreet. Not wanting their hair secrets unearthed, they'd either slip in through the back of the Max Factor building or the cosmetics wizard would send a wig specialist to the stars' homes for private fittings. Either way, Max had Hollywood covered—literally.

"It was a very glamorous and exciting time in my life, and I was thrilled to be part of his marvelous collection. The makeup not only made me look good, I felt very complimented to be chosen to represent the Max Factor brand. I enjoyed hearing Mr. Factor's stories of all the different stars and legends he'd attended to, and I'd finally met someone who was shorter than me—Mr. Factor himself!"
—Debbie Reynolds

An April 1, 1959 press photo taken on the company's fiftieth anniversary. The original photo caption read, "Cosmetologist Max Factor celebrates 50 years of making women beautiful with a three-tier cake and bevy of beautiful actresses. Left to right are actress Joi Lansing, Max Factor, actress Jayne Mansfield and actress Arlene Howell."

Chapter 11

KISS AND MAKEUP

THE PASSING OF A LEGEND

By the 1930s, Max Factor and Company had been running like a well-oiled machine for years. Factor's eldest son, Davis, was successfully overseeing domestic, as well as foreign, business affairs (including operations in Buenos Aires, London, Sydney and Paris); Louis Factor was in charge of manufacturing and packaging; and Sidney Factor ran the company's purchasing department. Frank Factor had worked alongside his father since boyhood and would later be an integral part of the development of Pan-Cake, as well as numerous other innovations

Unfortunately, Max Factor would never live to truly experience the success of the product he'd worked so hard to perfect with his son or the impact it would have for decades to come. While stepping off a curb in 1936, Max Factor was hit by a delivery truck. The accident is largely thought to have contributed—due to infection or other complications—to his death in 1938. The passing of the cosmetics pioneer would leave the family wondering what to do next, if only for a moment.

At the suggestion of Bill Hardwick (Hardwick had served as director of publicity for Max Factor and Company), and after contemplating which Factor would take over, it was decided that Frank, who had long displayed the same talent as his father had, would take the helm. Frank would legally change his name to Max Factor Jr. and seamlessly carry on the business his father had launched so many decades earlier. And filling the shoes of Max

Factor wouldn't be difficult. Max Jr. had already stockpiled a number of milestone innovations.

By the time the elder Factor had passed, the once-negative connotations surrounding makeup were gone, no longer hemming in the success of commercial cosmetics. Max Factor had gained widespread notoriety during his life, and now his son was ready to take over—but not before he made one final step to ensure the legacy of Max Factor and Company. The prolific Factor would have his hands insured for $500,000 (later, stars such as Betty Grable would follow suit, her studio insuring her legs for $1 million) and could confidently and effectively carry on the tradition. His first order of business would be lipstick.

THE PERFECT PUCKER

In 1939, in search of a lip color that stayed on, remained true to color and didn't cause chafing, Factor Jr. began working on a brand-new formula. In need of a fail-proof method for testing the indelibility of his latest product, he put word out for a pair of volunteers; two willing participants from the production department at one of the studios offered up their lips for the test. Some accounts have said that the volunteers were a married couple, while others have said they were married to other people—which is what would put an end to their volunteering. Whatever the case, the pair showed up on the first day. They applied lipstick, kissed and repeated with gusto, but eventually they would tire of the arduous task of test kissing and drop out. Finding another couple to replace them didn't prove to be so simple.

This led Factor Jr. to engineer a device so revolutionary that it would lay the groundwork for what is arguably one of the best lipstick formulas to date. Using his and hers rubber molds as the prototype for the groundbreaking apparatus, Factor's creation, dubbed "the Kissing Machine," would accomplish everything his smooch-weary human volunteers had and more. With its industrial black casing and mock crimson lips, the machine could gauge up to thirty pounds of pressure per kiss. While five pounds of pressure equaled a nice peck on the cheek (it was decided that thirty pounds was far too much pressure no matter what kind of kiss), ten pounds—five pounds from each kisser—proved to be the perfect amount. When a tissue was placed between the two sets of lips and the machine was activated, it achieved the ideal amount of pressure, proving that Factor's new lipstick was, in fact, indelible. Tru-Color Lipstick was officially launched in 1940—to the delight of Hollywood actresses and women all over the country.

With its natural look and smooth-as-silk finish, Pan-Cake had been engineered specifically for Technicolor film. Its meteoric rise to popularity started when stars began confiscating obscene amounts of it from the film set of *Vogues of 1938*. They'd loved its effect on the complexion for nighttime,

Pepsi and Pan-Cake: a publicity photo of Max Factor Jr. as he prepares for a cosmetics experiment.

but during the day, it was unsuitable to wear, as it made the face appear too dark. Though actresses had begged Max Sr. to create a formula for daytime, the cosmetician was staunchly opposed. Despite his son's urging him to make it available for daytime use—and to the public—Factor felt strongly that it should be reserved for use in motion pictures only.

Addressing the requests of hundreds of women, Max Jr. would finally design a daytime answer to the glorious Pan-Cake. In 1947, after years of experimentation—tests included covering models' legs in the makeup and then positioning them in the sun to observe how the color changed—Max Factor Jr. would introduce Pan-Stik. The wildly popular beautifying makeup in a stick form would be embraced by the glamorous set. It was trademarked in 1948, and like Pan-Cake, the simple-to-apply substance that yielded miraculous results immediately caught on like wildfire. Even better, Pan-Stik was designed to be applied "as easily as lipstick" in less than twenty seconds.

Factor's takeover of the role his father had so firmly established was flawless. He would continue to engineer the most technologically advanced and up-to-the-minute products to the delight of the hordes of movie stars and the female public. In the coming years, Factor Jr. would create Crème Puff, and in 1958, he would replace the former cake-and-brush method of eyelash makeup by bringing wand mascara to the public.

TELEVISION IN BLACK-AND-WHITE

Max Factor had grown up with the motion picture industry. But with the studio system in decline and the growing presence of television, which had started to catch on during the 1940s, things were beginning to change. The era of sending extras through extensive makeup and wardrobe fittings for lavish period films had passed. It had become too time-consuming and pricey. Studios looked to cut costs. What's more, cameras, lighting and other technology, as they'd done in previous years, had changed yet again. The presence of television in the 1950s would also signify the end of Max Factor's unheard-of one-dollar advertising deals with the stars. According to former television executive Tim Brooks, the advent of television brought with it spot advertising. Newer companies such as Revlon readily jumped on board with networks that enticed them with next-to-nothing airtime. With their images and careers no longer tied to a particular studio, actresses such as Janet Leigh, Debbie Reynolds and Elizabeth Taylor would be among the last of a fading away studio system to promote Max Factor and Company, and although stars with household names would still be featured in advertisements, it would never be done again the way it had been in the early years.

Not to be deterred, Max Factor and Company would begin a new era of marketing with advertisements that featured unknown (but beautiful nonetheless) print models. Changing times wouldn't prevent the cosmetics giant from engineering what would become some of the most popular products for television's new stars—and ultimately for the viewing public. In his research, Max Factor Jr. discovered a major discrepancy. Due to lack of compatibility where lighting and makeup were concerned, images, when projected in black-and-white television, created a frightening appearance on the actor's face. He knew the makeup would need to be reversed (dark hues must be applied underneath the eyes, below the cheeks and on laugh and smile lines, et cetera) in order to appear as a typical made-up face when transmitted onto television, but although reversing makeup worked on camera, off camera, the actor resembled a raccoon—not such a flattering look.

In 1946, Max Factor and Company would adapt Pan-Cake Makeup specifically for television, creating a flawless complexion and makeup appearance both on camera and off. In 1954, Max Factor Jr. created Erace (still available today), the first concealer designed to stamp out the appearance of blemishes, dark circles, wrinkles and all other unsightly flaws that could hamper the appearance of the face. In addition, the company would introduce its skin-perfecting Hi-Fi Fluid Makeup. Trumpeted as "doing for color what high fidelity had done for sound," the super-popular full-coverage makeup, which provided a natural dewy look, was available in myriad shades in order to suit every skin tone. And just as his father had done in the early years, Max Jr. would test his products first on his actresses; if they took a liking to the latest product, it was certain that women everywhere would follow suit—and they always did.

A NEW ERA

For the next nearly two decades—as recounted by Fred Basten—the company Max Factor would stop using the famous faces of movie stars to advertise its wares. The public would see a new crop of unknown models grace the company's print and television campaigns. No longer working exclusively with movies stars and their studios, the cosmetics conglomerate began hosting model searches and other contests—the Max Factor Girl contest among them—with thousands of dollars in prizes up for grabs, not to mention lots of publicity for a lucky winner. In the coming years, the longtime Hollywood-based brand would also highlight the carefree California lifestyle as it never had before, launching innumerable products that celebrated the land of sand, surf and sunshine. California Pink-a-Pades and California Sun Crèmes Lipsticks, California Blondes home hair color and California, the FiFi Award–winning fragrance created by legendary Max Factor spokesmodel Jaclyn Smith, were only a few of the irresistible cosmetics items introduced to the public, that made the Sunshine State the place everybody wanted to be.

The 1970s would signify a return to famous faces for the company. Cheryl Tiegs, Cheryl Ladd and Jane Seymour (in later decades, everyone from Whitney Houston, Beverly Johnson, Janice Dickinson and Carmen Electra to Gwyneth Paltrow and Madonna would represent the brand) would sign on to promote Max Factor. Despite how much makeup and style trends, as well as the needs and wants of everyday women, changed, the company stayed true to its roots, always upholding the golden-era glamour that the makeup guru had created some seven decades earlier.

Smith, whose looks embodied the Max Factor brand, would be the longest-running spokesmodel for the company, from the beginning of the 1970s through the end of the 1980s. Her run with the company rivals only that of Lucille Ball, who would promote the brand beginning in 1935 through the mid-1950s. Smith, who promoted hundreds of products (Pan-Stik, Skin Principle Moisturizer, Pure Magic Lipstick, Whipped Crème Makeup, Light and Natural Makeup, Epris perfume and scads of others), recalls her time representing Max Factor:

> *Max Factor really invented glamour, not just in the makeup, but in the image. When I was representing Max Factor, I remember that the colors really were really different from anything you find today—I think they were that way because he originally began creating makeup for cinema. You really don't get those kinds of colors anymore. From the time I first started doing campaigns for Max Factor during the '70s until I finished in the '80s, the entire idea of beauty and the way women wore makeup had totally changed. In the '70s, it was the low-slung bell-bottoms, and of course, it was all about the hair. Women weren't overly made up. The '70s were a very beautiful period—much more natural than the '80s. But Max Factor defined each decade, no matter how much the times changed.*

Max Factor demonstrating the rouge machine to popular Paramount contract player Rosalind Keith.

And even though the trends changed, there was always this return to the past and those classic looks that he first created for Hollywood. Many of the commercials I did were a nod to that era. As I recall in one campaign I did during the '80s, we referred to Jean Harlow and Marilyn Monroe and all of these iconic women. At the end of the commercial, we say, "Thanks Max!" Those glamorous women are still very much the prototype for today's ideal beauty.

Mannequin heads line the shelves of the extensive makeup department at the Max Factor Makeup Studio in 1928. A variety of character types reflect the trend of the historical drama that was popular throughout this era.

Opposite, top: Max Factor applies lipstick to Maria Osmena, daughter of Philippines vice president Sergio Osmena, while actress Evelyn Venable observes. Osmena was only one of the many women of nobility to visit the famed Hollywood showroom during its heyday.

Opposite, bottom: Max Factor posing with Margot Grahame and Ed Arnold. Before arriving in Tinsel Town, Grahame was Britain's highest-paid actress—as well as the country's answer to the famously platinum Jean Harlow—earning herself the moniker "the Aluminum Blonde."

Max Factor with Paramount star Carole Lombard.

Chapter 12

A BEAUTY RETROSPECTIVE

By the 1970s, Hollywood's golden era and the days of the studio system had long since passed. Max Factor was still a place where actors were sent by their managers and agents to have their "looks" analyzed, but by this time, most all of Hollywood had gone corporate. The landmark building that had served as the center of the beauty universe for nearly fifty years had begun to lose some of its luster. The glory days of film noir and Technicolor, of Tru-Color Lipstick and publicity photos had passed, and so had the days when movie studios lined up one-dollar deals with Max Factor to have the likes of Joan Crawford and Veronica Lake demonstrate the famed makeup in print advertisements that plugged their latest pictures. Times had changed in Hollywood, and it was inevitable that Max Factor and Company had to as well.

During the 1960s, the company reached the peak of its expansion, marketing to fourteen countries around the world. Although Davis Factor would serve as board chairman and Max Factor Jr. as vice-chairman of the board, many of the now third-generation family members who had been running the business had moved on to other pursuits. In 1973, a merger of Max Factor and Company and Norton Simon would take place, and it would prove to benefit both companies, as evidenced by Max Factor's soaring stock following Norton Simon's acquisition of the company.

Though the landmark art deco structure on Highland Avenue would continue as a makeup and hair salon, as well as a retail outlet, it would do so on a much smaller scale than it had in previous years. By 1983, yet another series of mergers would happen when Max Factor and Company was taken over by Beatrice Companies and, finally, by Playtex. Upon the merger, the company would relocate its corporate headquarters to the East Coast until 1986. It would be acquired a final time, and once a new company president was appointed, Max Factor's headquarters would return to the hallowed Hollywood and Highland location once again.

Gold Medal Memorabilia

The year 1984 would mark the seventy-fifth anniversary of Max Factor and Company. It would also coincide with another monumental event, the 1984 Olympic World Games, which were being held in Los Angeles that summer. In honor of both milestones, Max Factor executives asked Robert Salvatore to compile an exhibit at Max Factor in Hollywood. Veteran makeup artist and former Max Factor beauty director Salvatore had been with the company for decades and possessed a wealth of experience and knowledge. He had worked with all of the biggest stars and had gained the respect of everyone in the company. Salvatore would curate an exhibit for what would become the "Max Factor Museum of Beauty." The display of memorabilia was meant to be only temporary, but the public was so enthralled by it that the idea caught on. Slowly but surely, items were added to the collection. Before long, the museum was seeing upward of one thousand visitors each week.

The space that was once frequented by the biggest celebrities on the planet now housed a collection of beauty and movie memorabilia that dated back to 1904, when Max Factor first set up his exhibit at the St. Louis World's Fair. Although many parts of the now-dilapidated edifice were in need of refurbishing, many of its original features were still intact—from the ornate light fixtures and art deco display cases to the pulverizing and mixing machines—and the collection was something not to be missed. Testimonials from the likes of Clara Bow and Jaclyn Smith were included in the exhibit. Brillox Hair Oil, tubes of Supreme Greasepaint, publicity photos and original studio contracts signed by the stars, as well as hairpieces worn by the likes of Frank Sinatra, John Wayne and many others, made up some of the many items on display. The exhibit was slowly becoming something of a valuable collection. The space adjacent to the main showroom would become a retail outlet, where quality cosmetics, including Max Factor, Mary Quant, Halston, Orlane and others, could be purchased for a fraction of the usual cost. The Max Factor Museum of Beauty had started as a temporary exhibit and, in a short time, had caught on in a big way.

A much-needed break for the historic structure would come in 1990 with the filming of *The Two Jakes*. The film, set in 1947, called for a scene to be shot inside one of Max Factor's famed makeup rooms. It would earn the museum some additional publicity and a much-needed renovation at the suggestion of the film's star and director, Jack Nicholson. Paramount Studios would pony up $20,000 in order to restore the space to something that replicated its glorious art deco splendor. And it wasn't just a loose resemblance. Nicholson insisted that every display case be filled with the same makeup items one would have found inside them in October 1946. The renovation also included a magnificent restoration of reupholstered chaises, display cases and chandeliers from the art deco period.

Although Salvatore's museum would enjoy a successful thirteen-year run, the celebrated piece of living history would face an uncertain future—perhaps even the wrecking ball. All of Los Angeles was up in arms when it was announced that an indefinite closure on July 1, 1992, would take place. Historian Marc Wanamaker recalls the changing times:

All throughout the 1970s, the Max Factor building was still a presence in Hollywood. It was still a place stars would go, but nowhere near the way they'd done during the 1930s, '40s and '50s. In the 1970s, there were soap opera actors that would be sent over to Max Factor by their agents and managers to have their hair and makeup analyzed, so it was still known for such things at that time. But the 1970s were really the end of the era for the Max Factor days. In 1991, Proctor and Gamble bought Max Factor, but they had no interest in the building whatsoever. The Hollywood Heritage Museum had talked about buying the building, but that didn't end up happening for various reasons. There was the Hollywood Entertainment Museum, which had opened up down the street; they could have moved in to the space, but there was no way they were going to transfer the contents of their museum over to the Max Factor building.

As far as what was left inside, Proctor and Gamble had made plans to donate the collections to the Hollywood Entertainment Museum. Proctor and Gamble approached me and asked me to appraise all of the contents before everything was moved. When I went to do the appraisal, the place was empty. Nobody was there. I had the run of the building, so I wandered around. The lights were off. The rooms were empty. I could feel the history. Although it had been a working facility up through the 1970s, at the end, it had really become run down. Some of the fixtures were missing. Much of the stuff had been auctioned or sold to collectors. The four makeup rooms had become very shabby. The paint was peeling off the walls. There were lots and lots cosmetics cans and bottles and tubes and containers left lying around. There were also a lot of photo stills, beauty and packaging machines, booklets and brochures and that sort of thing. The place was all dirty, and it was all very sad. It sat empty for a year. When Donelle Dadigan bought it and announced that she planned to restore it, everyone was very happy because who knows what would have happened to it! In the beginning, she had a very small nucleus of items to put on show. Today, it's one of the best collections in the world.

PRESERVATION OF A HOLLYWOOD LANDMARK

When Proctor and Gamble took over in 1991, the company's decision to close the museum permanently had all of Los Angeles in a frenzy. Widespread protests were staged, urging everyone to save the beloved Max Factor building. Television news vans and media would occupy Highland Avenue daily as the saga dominated headlines. The overwhelming objection of the public would pay off in December 1993, when Proctor and Gamble announced it would grant an extension that would keep the museum in operation for three more years. Proctor and Gamble would then enter into an agreement with an undisclosed developer, with the stipulation that a $1.5 million memorabilia museum would be built, though funds had yet to be allocated at that time. Eventually, however, all such arrangements would fall through. By the time the three-year reprieve was up, the building would sit empty indefinitely—closed to the public and not for sale. But it hadn't gone unnoticed.

Philanthropist and real estate developer Donelle Dadigan had been paying attention to the situation. In 1994, Dadigan and her mother would purchase the Max Factor building from Proctor and Gamble for $1.15 million, closing escrow on Halloween day. A delighted Dadigan, who recalls, "To this day, I still can't understand how we were so fortunate to be able to rescue this building," would strive to create a place for motion picture and beauty enthusiasts alike, as well as for the droves of tourists coming to Hollywood hoping to connect with the larger-than-life movie stars of a time that is no longer.

Dadigan would invest more than $8 million to restore the Max Factor building back to its original art deco grandeur. To ensure the renovations were as authentic as possible, the same architectural plans that had been drafted by S. Charles Lee during the 1930s were used. An avid collector herself, Dadigan, who launched the Hollywood Museum in 2003, would build on her personal assortment of memorabilia, creating what would eventually become one of the most extensive collections in the world. Today, the thirty-five-thousand-square-foot entertainment industry tribute remains homage to the makeup guru and the golden era he created. The Hollywood Museum spans more than a century of movie history and has more than ten thousand items on show within its vast collection. Among its many treasures, the Hollywood Museum houses the largest authentic collection of Marilyn Monroe memorabilia in the world, including the actress's curvaceous measurements—something she was known for being evasive about—the sequined spaghetti strap dress she wore to entertain the troops during the Korean War and the 1961 Cadillac Fleetwood that was gifted to her by producer Darryl Zanuck.

In 2009, Max Factor and Company would say farewell to the United States permanently (though the trendsetting color cosmetics are still available online) when its parent company, Proctor and Gamble, relocated all future business dealings to Europe. Today, the time-honored landmark is a favorite of historians, memorabilia collectors, movie enthusiasts and lovers of vintage beauty alike. It will forever be the place where Hollywood magic was manufactured. It's the place where, in an effort to convince Otto Perminger to cast her as the star of *Carmen Jones*, Dorothy Dandridge would run from Perminger's office over to Max Factor, sharing with one reporter, "I hurried to Max Factor's stuido and looked around for the right garb. I found an old wig. I found a shaggy but brilliant blouse, I arranged it off the shoulder. Then I located a provocative skirt. I put on heavy lipstick, worked spit curls around my face. I would return looking like Carmen herself."

It was the birthplace of shimmer eye shadow, tube lipstick and wand mascara; the place where Max Factor and his lab coat–wearing technicians ceremoniously painted the famed zigzag lightning bolt stripes across Sally Rand's birthday suit in Technicolor makeup. It's where Marilyn Monroe regularly went to get her famous flaxen curls coiffed; and where Katharine Hepburn, Marlene Dietrich, Barbara Stanwyck, Jane Russell, Loretta Young and a host of other glamour dolls would frequent so often, it was nearly their second home. It was where women in search of the same smooth-as-silk skin as the famous faces they so admired would phone and write from all over the world requesting the illustrious Pan-Cake Makeup for themselves. The former Max Factor Makeup Studio is still a place worthy of the most glamorous of glamour puss; it's a place where one can gain inspiration, a look back into the past and a glimpse inside the enduring legacy of Max Factor.

Max Factor with feather-festooned Sally Rand in 1937.

L O O K   Y O U R   L O V L I E S T
A T   A N Y   A G E

IF YOU ARE 16 to 20

Complexion care and the emphasis of colour and features are all-important to this age group. If your skin is healthy, cleanse your face with cream or lotion, then wash with a mild soap and water. Always rinse thoroughly and pat dry. If you are troubled with adolescent skin irritations, seek the advice of a dermatologist, for neglected adolescent skin can result in scars. Emphasize eyebrows by removing stray hairs from between them and over the eyelids. Brush eyebrows regularly with an eyebrow brush. Wear pastel shades of lipstick, learn to use a lipstick brush so you can apply lipstick perfectly. For a pale face, a touch of rouge gives a healthy look. Guard against wearing too much make-up. Apply only a touch of foundation and a light dusting powder in a shade that matches your skin colouring. If skin tends to spots and blackheads, use Astringent Foundation. Youngest members of this age group should eliminate the foundation and use only a light application of Face Powder or Crème Puff.

IF YOU ARE 20 to 30

This age group demands more mature grooming and make-up. Techniques of make-up should have been perfected by now, for unskilled applications can look bizarre on this still youthful group. Emphasize your most attractive features and subdue those which are unattractive. With make-up, learn how to reduce the size of a nose that is too prominent; how to make closely set eyes look farther apart; how to make a long face look shorter, a wide face look more oval, and a thin face look wider. In other words, learn how to make an imperfect face look more perfect. Make-up fads can be worn by this age group better than any other, for when unusual colours and make-up patterns are applied to young, firm faces, it is obvious that they are being worn for fashion and effect. However, real beauty is natural, so accept the fads for the moment and with discretion. Then drop them the day they begin to wane, or they might become a habit and make you look dated.

IF YOU ARE **30** to **40**

This age group is often considered the most beautiful. It is the time when a woman can combine her maturity and make-up skill to make the most of her beauty. Dramatic effects with make-up may be achieved for certain occasions, and may be carried with the character and poise of the truly mature woman. Every woman of this age should guard against a "too young" look in make-up and make-up colours. These are the years when a woman must concentrate more than ever on the care of her skin, for much of the beauty she will retain throughout her life depends on this care. Cleanse the skin more perfectly. Lubricate the skin every twenty-four hours, without fail. Tone the skin with Freshener or Astringent. Protect the skin with lanolin-laden foundations every hour of the day. With an eye on the future, many women start using Secret Key to get the fullest possible benefit from their beauty routine.

IF YOU ARE **40** to **50**

Women of this age group may experience their first signs of grey hair. This is nature's way of providing softness for the entire face. So if your hair hair is grey, or turning grey, it is your cue to wear softer make-up tones, less rouge. Never wear unusual shades of make-up foundations, but match them perfectly to your skin. Apply your eyebrow pencil more delicately and use a softer shade of eyelash make-up, if you have been accustomed to using black. Select the light shades of lipstick and rouge, which are in your colour range and apply them with a deft hand. Do not follow make-up fads, but adhere to the most natural applications. You should use every beauty requisite you have always used, for if they are applied more subtly, you should appear as you did during the 30 to 40 period. Continue the rigid care of your skin. If you are not turning grey, however, be doubly sure to apply your make-up in the soft, natural shades with even greater care.

IF YOU ARE **50 PLUS**

This age group can be lovely and most attractive. However, there are certain rules to follow: DO not use too much rouge in any attempt to look younger. Some women discard many of their beauty requisites and then, in trying to look younger, apply too much rouge, achieving an artificial painted effect. Take care in applying lipstick, too, to avoid the appearance of a drooping mouth. Wear only the soft, pastel shades. Do not use face powder or foundation too light or too dark for your skin, or you will look obviously made up. Select colours that harmonize with your skin tones. If your eyebrows or eyelashes are turning white, or have turned white, tint them delicately with eyebrow pencil and eyelash make-up. Do not give up any of your make-up requisites. Use them more sparingly as you grow older, but use them with all the skill you have learned over the years. Or, if you have never before used make-up, remember it is never too late to start!

*From the 1954 Max Factor and Company product booklet You at Your Lovliest.

BIBLIOGRAPHY

Academy of Motion Picture Arts and Sciences Margaret Herrick Library. Research Collection. http://www.oscars.org/library.

Basten, Fred E. *Max Factor: The Man Who Changed the Faces of the World.* New York: Arcade Publishing, 2008.

Bison Archives. Images. http://www.bisonarchives.com.

Bennett, James. Cosmetics and Skin. www.cosmeticsandskin.com.

Chanzanov, Mathis. "Museum of Beauty Rescued from Ugly Prospect of Closure." *Los Angeles Times*, December 10, 1992. http://articles.latimes.com/1992-12-10/local/me-2378_1_hollywood-museum.

Discover Los Angeles. "LA Story Spotlight: Donelle Dadigan." May 9, 2014. http://www.discoverlosangeles.com/blog/la-story-spotlight-donelle-dadigan.

Fort Lee Film Commission. http://www.fortleefilm.org.

Los Angeles Times Syndicate. "Max Factor's Beauty Museum Prepares to Fade Away." *Baltimore Sun*, June 18, 1992. http://articles.baltimoresun.com/1992-06-18/features/1992170237_1_max-factor-koss-hollywood-entertainment-museum.

Max Factor International. http://maxfactor-international.com.

TCM Films. *Starring Dorothy Dandridge.* http://www.tcm.com

University of Wisconsin–Madison. Department of Communication Arts. www.mediahistoryproject.org.

PERSONAL INTERVIEWS

Adkins, Richard, president, Hollywood Heritage Museum.
Brooks, Tim, former television executive, television historian.
Dadigan, Donelle, owner and founder, Hollywood Museum, 2013.
Reynolds, Debbie.
Smith, Jaclyn.
Wanamaker, Marc.

INDEX

ABOUT THE AUTHOR

Erika Thomas writes for the lifestyle publications *Southern California Life*, *Los Angeles Confidential*, *Chevrolet New Roads* and others. A former actress, Erika made the rounds at Paramount, Warner Bros. and the Culver Studios (her drive-on pass often taking her through the Ince Gate), where she was always more interested in the history of the famed structures than she was in booking the acting job itself. She holds a degree in English and creative writing from California State University–Northridge. Her love of golden-era Hollywood began at the age of nine, when she saw a rerun of the 1959 film *Some Like It Hot*. Since then, she's been an enthusiast of old school haunts that

range from Lana Turner's booth at Formosa Café and Liz Taylor's bungalow at the Beverly Hills Hotel to every Googie-era bowling alley and coffee shop in between. Erika enjoys writing about Southern California history, architecture and design.